JOURNEY TO
THE FINAL CAST

*A Memoir of Fishing, Friendship,
and Growing Old*

Glenn Busch

Journey to the Final Cast

© 2011

Glenn Busch

ISBN: 978-1-936553-23-5

Glenn Busch
3024 Cardinal Place
Lynchburg, VA 24503
(434) 384-8673
glenn.busch@gmail.com

Cover by Gazehound Design

Warwick House Publishers
720 Court Street
Lynchburg, VA 24504

To my fishing buddies:
the ones who are gone
and those who remain,
especially my grandson James
and his little brother Matthew.

CONTENTS

A GALLERY OF GEEZERS

If the magazine-cover exploits of young and middle-age fishermen are what usually hook your reading interests, this book offers an alternative—perhaps unique—perspective. This is an unashamed, unabashed, and uncensored collection of angling adventures generated by a group of geezers who began compiling their fishing vitae before many of today's seasoned river guides had learned to walk.

The men wandering through these pages were well into adulthood before carbon fibers ever found their way into fishing rods. Each one can remember fishing with fiberglass, or even bamboo, before that elegant material became an expensive symbol of status. They remember when the fly-fishing section occupied no more than a few scant pages in the L.L. Bean and Orvis catalogs. They have memories of pulling on clunky canvas waders and cranking stiff level line onto old Pflueger reels.

The men in these stories grew up when most landowners were fine about your crossing their fields on your way to the water, just so long as you remembered to shut the gates. And all of them did. They knew about not letting out the horses and cattle, but more especially about being courteous to your neighbors and friends. They grew up before there was so much posting of land and lived through that glorious era when you could fish just about anywhere you cared to…and there were plenty of places to choose from.

Specifically, this is a book about a group of friends who have known one another for decades—some since childhood—buddies who not only fish together but have grown old together.

There are nine members in this cast of characters, including one who is deceased. All are over sixty; the oldest is seventy-seven. Every one has grown children, and most have grandchildren, too.

We live in Virginia, West Virginia, and North Carolina. Most of us are native Southerners, except for the three transplanted Yankees from Pennsylvania, Ohio, and Wisconsin, but even they have lived in the South so long—their entire professional careers—that they, too, consider it home.

About half are retired, and the rest are at most a few years away. There are two CPAs, an outdoor writer, a dermatologist, two optometrists, a business executive, a substance abuse specialist, and an Episcopal priest. And our personalities and temperaments are as varied as our work.

A few enjoy art, theater, classical music and difficult books. Most listen to bluegrass, love their dogs, and own a truck. Some are churchgoers, and some are not. One chews tobacco (two others gave it up), and all of us have been known to take a drink.

Our political views swing widely with two decided liberals, an archconservative, and the rest who land a degree or two to the right or left of center. Notwithstanding some testy discussions, especially during election season, none of this has ever interfered with the friendships or the fishing.

We all drag behind us long histories that testify to multiple experiences of joy, sorrow, frustration, and accomplishment—in life as well as sport. And each one of us can recount stories of personal difficulties and periods of particularly hard times. Four divorced and later remarried; two are cancer survivors; one had a serious bout of depression; and all have experienced conflicts, crises, uncertainty, disappointment, and problems with family, jobs, and health.

As a group, we are more spread out than we used to be: Careers and retirement took us to new and different places. But we still get together regularly, we still enjoy one another's company, and we have as much fun together as we ever did…probably more.

Like the Tennessee whiskey that awaits us at the end of a day on the water, we have mellowed with age. We don't measure success by the number of fish we catch. Although we all can remember a time when we did.

Such competitive intrusions don't plague us anymore. Now we even take satisfaction in the angling success of another. And a bad day on the water more than likely is determined by some circumstance that required us to return home early.

Patience is more evident among us. No one seems to be in a rush anymore. We pause to enjoy the scenery, to take in the smell of honeysuckle in the spring and the sight of luminous leaves lighting up the Appalachian Mountains in the fall. The conversation, the food, even the drive to the water are essential parts of the whole when we think about what it means to "go fishing."

While it's a fact that a few of us fish less than we used to, it is also a fact that others actually fish more, now that we have the extra time. Let that be an incentive to generations our junior. Dream, we want to tell them, dream—as we used to—about a time when you will be less encumbered by the restraints of responsibility. Such dreams are worth indulging because they often do come true. They have for us, and we hope that the exploits of these nine fishing geezers will convince you, too.

CREATURE COMFORTS

Honesty requires that this account begin with an acknowledgment: Certain adjustments—let us call them creature comfort allowances—were made by us geezers as the years progressed.

In the early days, we took a semiannual trip into the Cranberry Backcountry in West Virginia. Looking back on those expeditions from the perspective of thirty years makes them seem like boot camp. But it didn't seem so then. We loved those trips, and the dates were more sacrosanct on our calendars than a national holiday or a family celebration. For weeks in advance we would begin collecting gear, purchasing food, and contacting one another about meeting plans, arrangements, and supplies.

Because the Cranberry River flowed through a designated wilderness area, no motorized vehicles were permitted. Everything we needed had to be carried in: tents, food, cooking utensils, fishing gear, extra clothes, sleeping bags, the works. After a two- to three-mile hike, we would set up camp—which took a couple of hours—before we dispersed along the river to fish.

We fished hard on those trips, as young men do: up early, to bed late. We slept on the ground, kept warm and told stories by the campfire, cooked over an open flame, and did without a shower for the duration of the trip. When it was all over, we reversed the process and arrived home exhausted but ready for work the next day. It was a test of endurance, but none of us complained. To us the enjoyment was unequaled, even the time it rained so hard our camp was awash in mud.

Some years later, partly due to better sense and improved financial circumstances, but more because we were well past middle age and more aware of bodily discomforts and minor afflictions, we decided it might be worthwhile to pursue a less muscular form of camping.

Jim, an outdoor writer with the wherewithal to put us onto new fishing venues, suggested one fall that we try the Jackson River in Virginia instead of the Cranberry. The Jackson option, he said, would allow us to park our vehicles within a few hundred yards of a riverside campsite. No more long hikes carrying gear like pack animals.

The idea met with immediate enthusiasm and fit nicely with the realization that because almost all of us now owned trucks, we could increase the tonnage of the gear we took along. Which we most certainly did.

We purchased larger tents—much larger tents. One was the size of a small condominium and may have given the impression that the circus had arrived. In some respects, that may not have been an altogether false conclusion.

We also purchased an expansive tarp to cover a new camp kitchen with all the accouterments of an Army mess. We built an oversize Dutch oven out of a stovepipe, rocks, and a large rectangle of quarter-inch steel. And because we had all that space in the beds of so many trucks, we added lounge chairs, air mattresses, and a half cord of firewood. Why scrounge for wood in the forest when you can bring your own?

Wayne, one of the two CPAs in our group, built a portable toilet with armrests attached. Such luxury afforded the opportunity to sit and read while taking care of business.

Then there was the food. Because we could now bring along those large plastic coolers that can double as a bench for two broad-butted adults, we brought several and filled them full. Jim, unrivaled as a camp cook, assumed his duties with culinary vigor. He served us shrimp cocktails to accompany our pre-dinner drinks. We dined on pork loin, beef medallion, and smoked trout. And the feast would conclude with all of us sprawled on the lounge chairs, sipping Kahlua and cream, as we dozed by the roaring fire. And, yes, we fished, too.

The vagaries of nature instigated our next notable transformation. One October, after we had been camping along the Jackson for more than a decade, a severe drought caused the Forest Service to forbid any type of open fire, which scuttled our style of camp cooking. And can you picture camping without a campfire? We couldn't.

Once again, Jim came up with a solution so we wouldn't have to cancel the trip. He knew the owner of a nearby hunting preserve who would rent us one of his lodges. We agreed…"but just this once."

Our wives, however, were more alert to our vulnerability to seduction. Dave—an optometrist who once held the Virginia record for rainbow trout—remembers his wife and mine predicting, as they observed how lightly we packed for our stay in *a lodge*, that we might as well go ahead and sell our tents because we wouldn't be needing them anymore.

We laughed politely and dismissed their cynicism. "It's just this one time, until the open-fire ban is lifted," we reminded them. Today, neither Dave nor I can remember for sure what we did with those tents.

We have returned to the lodge every spring and fall since. We drive up to the front door, take a few minutes to carry a duffel bag or two to one of the bedrooms, catch up with one another on the deck or in the fireplace room, then drive to one of several streams in the area. Which still includes the Jackson.

Occasionally, when we are over that way, we stop by the old campsite, for old times' sake. The last time we were there, a few remnants of the old Dutch oven were still tucked in the hillside cave where we hid them, nearly fifteen years ago.

Nowadays when we return to the lodge after a day on the water, we mix a drink at our well-stocked bar, eat Jim's gourmet cooking around a massive dining room table, put our dirty plates in the dishwasher, and fall into a comfortable double bed when it's time to retire. It's not the same as it was on the Cranberry and Jackson trips, but there is some compensation in having a warm shower and a dry toilet.

HEAVY ORDNANCE

Dave and I have been fishing buddies for more than thirty years. In the course of our companionable fishing life, we have spent hundreds of dollars getting skunked in famous places; been chased by a bull; nearly slid off the side of a mountain while driving on ice-covered roads; endured a day imprisoned on a johnboat with a nonstop-talking New York fishing guide who provoked even our gentle spirits to contemplate the consequences of homicide; driven through post-hurricane flooding; and found ourselves in the wee hours of the morning at the emergency room in Bozeman, Montana.

It is too bad that bonus points aren't awarded—like frequent flyer miles—for distance covered while wading rivers and streams. Dave and I would qualify for a piscatorial gold card. From the Catskills to Yellowstone, an ocean of water has passed between our legs.

Most of the time we catch fish. Occasionally we don't. But somehow we always manage to wrest a good time out of whatever happens.

You might attribute that good fortune to some shared philosophy, such as "maintaining a positive attitude" or "looking for the best in people." But that isn't it. We rarely talk philosophy—not the classical type anyway. And when you have fished together as long as we have, you are bound to have run into some real jerks about whom little more can be said than "What an asshole." All we can say for sure is that we have been friends for years and one good time has been a prelude to the next.

For the past three years, Dave and I have hired a guide and floated a section of the New River in Southwest Virginia lauded for its trophy smallmouth bass. One more year of this and we can declare it a binding tradition, therefore making it unnecessary to justify the expense— sort of like a government entitlement or an anniversary celebration. At least we hope our wives will see it that way. Is it really any different from, say, a commitment to a religious institution or paying college tuition?

The sky was cloudy and overlaid with a touch of fog on the morning of our most recent trip to the New. As we pulled out of Dave's driveway, the radio weather guy announced favorable conditions, especially for fishing: cloud cover, not too hot (July in the South can fry you like an egg), with a *slight*—I know he said slight—chance of scattered afternoon thundershowers.

The report from the guide and others we talked to was that the fish were really on. So, with those auspicious indicators before us, we set off with high expectations— two graying versions of Tom Sawyer and Huck Finn in search of fish and adventure on the ancient New River, one of the oldest rivers in the world.

The sky darkened as we turned west toward Blacksburg, and scary-looking clouds the color of old lead started to congregate like a gang of thugs looking for a fight. But we placed our confidence in the weatherman and remained optimistic.

By the time we met up with the guide and hauled the boat to the put-in ramp, the weather looked like a bad day in London. There wasn't a patch of blue to be found, and rain fell with such determination that we took refuge under a nearby bridge.

Our guide used his cell phone to call a friend with access to a weather radar screen. The friend reported back that we were in the middle of a large mass of precipitation that appeared to be moving off, with clear skies behind. He calculated that it would take about an hour for it to pass.

By eleven o'clock, it was obvious that the rain liked the scenery and had decided to stall and visit for a while. And because we were paying good money to huddle under the bridge with our guide, we decided to climb into the drift boat and shove off anyway.

The rain slackened an hour or so later, pumping up our spirits as we offered one another wishful words of encouragement.

"Doesn't it look a lot brighter over there? I mean, less gray than it was?"

"Oh yeah, definitely. It's getting ready to clear up."

We drifted and fished for another half mile or so before the rain, like a runner getting a second wind, resumed its vigorous pace, forcing us to pull over and take refuge under the branches of some overhanging trees. But there is only so much shelter trees can offer under a constant, heavy pelting.

Heat and sun being what we had expected, we were dressed accordingly in lightweight shirts and pants. We had also brought along rain jackets…just in case.

The trees and rain jackets did a respectable job up top, but soon we were soaked from the waist down. Dave, in skimpy, lightweight shorts, began to shiver. The guide tossed him a pair of old waders to slip into, then busied himself bailing out the boat. I spent my time trying to find a comfortable way to sit, now that my undershorts were wet and my butt was getting sore. All of us were beyond impressed with how cold rain could be in the middle of July.

The rain gave us one more good drenching before finally moving on, having taken four hours to vacate instead of the predicted one. But, happy to be fishing again, we pushed the boat back out into the main current and resumed casting large, black cicada patterns along the wooded banks.

Patches of blue replaced the fleeting clouds, and it wasn't long before we felt like picnic steaks broiling in the heat of the naked sun. We sweated. Our wet clothes steamed. We swilled bottled water. And we caught a few fish. Things were looking up.

The stretch of the New River we like best meanders through a government facility known as the Radford Army Ammunition Plant, where military ordnance is manufactured and tested. It is a huge facility that runs for nearly ten miles on both sides of the river. And except for the occasional stilted guard tower that pokes above the trees, little of it can be seen from a boat floating by.

Drifting through this section of the river is permitted, but you better not stop and step on land. "NO TRESPASSING" signs are posted along both banks. We have been told—but I can't confirm—that hidden cameras watch the river and those on it at all times. Which ordinarily poses no problem. We float through, fish from the boat, and aside from hearing a distant rumble once in awhile, hardly even notice that the armory is there. But not on this trip.

Around midafternoon, during that short period when the sun blessed us with its presence, an ear-splitting siren went off. It was followed by an authoritative voice from some unseen public address system—I instantly thought of the Wizard of Oz—that issued this stern announcement: "The armory is about to do a burn."

"Burn," we were about to learn, is official speak for *We are about to blow the hell out of something.*

The disembodied voice issued a follow-up command. And this was the part that *really* got our attention: "For your own safety, evacuate the river...now!"

"I've never heard that before," our guide said. Which seemed ominous when you consider that he is on the river six days a week from April through October. But because there were no other boats, fishermen, or other human beings anywhere in sight, we concluded that The Voice must be speaking to us.

The three of us looked at one another in wondering silence. Where did The Voice expect us to evacuate *to*? We were in a drift boat. The banks were posted government property, which conjured images of guards, guns, and mean-ass dogs. We didn't seem to have many options and hoped that The Voice, who was watching us from God knows where, would soon pick up on that.

There being no further instructions from The Voice, we floated on, our guide keeping us on a steady, straight-downriver course. We drifted no more than a hundred yards when a mighty explosion accompanied by a roiling, three-story ball of fire made a grand display on the far bank. I have seen film footage of Navy jets blowing up suspected terrorist targets that was less spectacular. Or maybe it just seemed so. Being in the general vicinity of the real thing is bound to have some effect on your perceptions.

Dave and I remain grateful to The Voice for giving us a heads up. Otherwise, we just might have crapped in our soggy shorts. We also considered the possibility that The Voice got a good look at us through one of those hidden cameras and decided that the Army didn't need two geezer heart attack victims on its hands.

A dense, orange cloud then formed where the fireball flamed out, concentrating into what looked like a mammoth mound of fuzzy cotton. As it oozed slowly skyward, our guide asked the question that was on all our minds: "What do you think is in that stuff?"

Dave and I laughed our best manly indifference, but continued watching the progress of the orange monster out of the corner of our eyes as thoughts of deadly carcinogens danced through our minds. When the prevailing breeze pushed it farther and farther away, our gluteus muscles finally relaxed.

With the excitement seemingly behind us, the sun shining, and our clothes nearly dry, a confident attitude of routine fishing returned. There was no reason to expect any further adversities to descend upon us. After all, the day and the float were nearly spent. What else could happen in the short time that remained?

About a mile from the takeout point, we noticed a dark mass moving in from downriver. Periodic flashes of lightning ripped through towering black clouds, and a wide band of solid rain marched out in front of them.

This storm was clearly meaner and uglier than the one that passed through earlier in the day.

Hoping that we could reach the takeout point before the storm was upon us, we reeled in and our guide hauled on the oars.

"Do you think we can beat it?" Dave asked.

"I hope so," our guide puffed as he labored to increase our downstream speed.

He put forth a valiant effort, but the storm outran us. Within minutes of contact, it felt as though we were sitting beneath Niagara Falls. The wind picked up, too, strong enough to form whitecaps on the river's roiling surface. When thunder and lightning followed, we knew we had to head for shore.

We beached the boat, moved back from the river's edge, and clustered in a spot we thought least likely to tempt a lightning strike. The riverbanks turned to sludge during the deluge, and for a while the rain fell so heavy and thick we couldn't see to the other side. There was little else to do but stand and wait it out.

From under his rain hood, droplets cascading from the end of his nose, Dave offered a helpful suggestion: "Let's have a beer." Which, given the circumstances, I heartily endorsed.

Our guide slogged over to the boat, pulled three beers out of the cooler, and handed them around. Hoisting mine skyward through the downpour, I offered a tribute to the day: "Ah, this is the life, isn't it?" Our youthful guide flashed one of those looks that children give their aging parents when they are beginning to suspect the onset of senility. But I was sure that Dave understood.

The storm blew out as quickly as it blew in, we clambered back in the boat, and drifted the remaining half mile that would conclude the trip. Dave put up his rod and sat for the rest of the ride. I stood, but not to fish. My undershorts were wet again, and I was hoping to avoid a case of chapped cheeks. I hate that.

We helped get the boat securely on the trailer, changed out of our wet clothes, and settled up with the guide. The fishing—the catching part of it, anyway—had been poor when we had any at all. But Dave summed up the day nicely for both of us. "That was fun. Let's schedule this trip again next year."

ED'S BENCH

When the phone rings at odd hours in our house, bad news often awaits at the other end. The early morning call, just days before Christmas, was no exception.

It was Dave at the other end. Ed died last night, he said. He's the first of our group to go. The sad news bored into my head and settled in my heart.

It is a generalization, but I'll make the claim none-theless. There is a special bond among men who love to fish and be outside, and our group has a bond as tight as old cement.

Ed was one of us. He reveled in the same experiences that brought all of us together in the first place: throwing horseshoes and a lot of bull at the end of a long day on the stream, gathering around a campfire and telling ribald tales and bad jokes, the taste of camp coffee in the morn-ing, the musty smell of a damp forest floor, the sounds of nature waking up in the hours just before dawn, and a deep appreciation for old trucks and a good dog.

Ed was one of us, and now he was gone. Just before hanging up the phone, Dave expressed the very sentiment I was about to convey to him: It'll never be the same.

A few hours later, I received a call from Ed's wife. She allowed as to how she knew it was a busy time of the year for me, "with Christmas only a couple of days away and all," but could I possibly come to Roanoke and officiate at Ed's funeral, she wanted to know. Two days later, a day before Christmas Eve, I was on the road to Virginia to bury my friend.

God only knows how many funerals I have conducted over a thirty-six-year career as an Episcopal parish priest. Plenty. And I know all the techniques necessary to keep my emotions in check, but it was still tough getting through Ed's service.

After it was over, several of us stopped by Ed's house to speak to his family. We ate a quick lunch from the buffet table provided by family friends, said a final goodbye to Ed's widow, and made our exit. We wished one another a merry Christmas, got in our cars, and headed our separate ways.

Four months would pass before our group was back together again for the annual spring fishing trip. It would be the first time we were together...without Ed.

Most of the men I know are not viscerally expressive when it comes to managing grief and sadness. Whether it is a result of the prevailing attitude of male behavior during the era in which we were raised, or some other reason, that's the way we are. And try as we sometimes do to convey more *feeling*, we remain at least partially captive to a form of emotional stoicism that defines the manner in which we share our sorrows.

The need to express what is locked inside remains nonetheless, which is surely one reason for poetry, song, ritual, worship, and sympathy cards. Such practical devices enable us to unleash, from one step removed, sentiments too powerful, too threatening to discharge in a form that is raw, keenly personal, and undisguised.

We had already decided, well in advance of the spring trip, to conduct our own private memorial service in honor of Ed. In addition, we all agreed that we needed something tangible that would serve as a permanent marker of Ed's presence among us. After discussing numerous possibilities, we finally settled on a stone bench to which a plaque would be affixed.

Ed was the quiet member of our group who valued his time alone. He particularly enjoyed sitting in a lounge chair outside our rented lodge, sipping a drink, and looking down on the nearby pond where he had fished earlier in the day. He loved the sights and sounds of the natural world that are so abundant and so incomparably beautiful in the mountainous region of Bath County, Virginia. A bench, we all agreed, would be a fitting memorial: We could imagine Ed sitting there, even when he wasn't.

Jim and John volunteered to purchase the bench. Wayne said he would get the plaque. I was the obvious choice to take responsibility for the service.

On the day we arrived for the spring trip, we settled into our rooms and made plans to hold Ed's memorial service that evening, just before dinner. We fished a little during the afternoon, but everyone was back at the lodge well before the agreed-upon hour.

We congregated just outside the front door of the lodge, on a grassy knoll that overlooks an expansive woodland field. At that spot, we had spent many evenings together with Ed, bent forward in our chairs, peering through a telescope at the deer and wild turkeys foraging in the field, or watching ripples form on the pond below.

The evening was spring-beautiful: budding trees, wildflowers in early bloom, the scent of pine and last year's moldering leaves. Jim and John got us started by carrying the heavy concrete bench from the bed of John's truck and carefully setting it in place. We then formed a loose circle, and I passed around some printed material we would use during our brief memorial.

An accurate recollection of what we actually said and did is lost to me now, no doubt obscured by the poignancy of the occasion. I do remember that we read passages from Scripture, said a few prayers, and made some extemporaneous tributes to Ed before finally saying "Amen." In a somber mood we went inside and sat down to dinner, where an unplanned part of our memorial was about to begin.

Maybe it was the fact that we were sitting around a table. Anyone with even the slightest acquaintance with religious symbols knows that tables are the preeminent places in religious literature where truth and intimacy break out. We may just as well have been influenced by the wine and whiskey. Whatever the reason, the conversation around the dinner table was healing balm. Paroled from our emotional cages, we opened up and spoke unfettered words about Ed and all that he had meant to us.

We told one Ed story after another as the dinner segued into an impromptu wake where we ate and laughed and reminisced about the time Ed fell out of the tree; the time Ed passed out in the wood cart; the time Ed …. With food and fellowship, we fashioned a homely sacramental way of saying a proper and cleansing farewell to our fishing buddy Ed.

The next day, Wayne got out his tools, and he and George spent a lot more time than was really necessary carefully measuring and marking and drilling and inserting the screws that would attach the memorial plaque to Ed's bench. Anyone who sits there, or merely passes by, will see its simple inscription: In Memory of Ed Barbery — Dedicated April 23, 2003.

Many fishing trips have come and gone since then. But each time we gather at the lodge, those of us who remain think about the old times and all that has happened to us since we first got together as a group. We are old enough now to appreciate the wisdom of the old adage about pursuing the really important things in life.

It is good to have a special place to meditate on matters such as that. There is a particularly good spot for meditation in Bath County, Virginia, where it's quiet and terrific natural scenery is all around. Just take a seat on Ed's bench, and I am sure you will agree.

JUSTICE SERVED

The affections of men run a strange course. The deeper the friendship, the more likely we are to verbally harass one another in ways we would not think of inflicting on a mere acquaintance, or even a perfect stranger for that matter. Unless one were to cut us off in traffic or make fun of our dog, but that's different.

Dave refers to these barbed interchanges as giving someone "a ration of shit." It's all in good fun: jocular banter, sometimes profane, mixed with practical jokes that add to the male bonding and camaraderie.

A good laugh for all the participants is the intent; but there are boundaries. Our group has been at it long enough to know what they are, and we don't exceed them. Deliberately trying to offend or hurt someone's feelings is not part of the game; and besides, we have too much respect and genuine affection for one another for that to be even a potential risk.

On one trip that included a little squirrel hunting on the side, Dave bagged enough for our group to enjoy a big pot of squirrel stew. For months thereafter, I would find squirrel tails in items I had taken on the trip. Taking a walk with my wife one evening, I reached inside the pocket of my jacket to fetch a pair of gloves. Gloves were not what I came out with. At the time, I could only be amused by the thought of how much craft and deception

Dave had employed in planting all those tails in my gear without my noticing.

On another occasion, professional duties kept me from being on time for one of our group trips, so I asked the boys to pick up my fishing license when they purchased theirs. They said they would take care of it.

The day I arrived, I was in a big hurry to make up for lost time. I rushed to the river and was fishing only twenty or so yards from our campsite when a West Virginia State Trooper—whom I mistook for a game warden—asked to see my license. I explained the circumstances, that my friends had bought my license for me and I had yet to get it from them, but if he "would be so kind as to walk with me right over there to the campsite… "

He interrupted and began giving me a stern lecture about how it was my responsibility to have a license in my possession at all times.

"Yes, officer," I pleaded, "but if you will just let me go right over there, I will… "

"No," he said, "the law requires that you have your license on your person while fishing."

"I understand, officer, but… "

This probably would have gone on longer, but guffawing from behind the bushes erupted. I knew then that my friends were somehow instigators of what was beginning to look like my impending arrest.

It turned out that the whole thing was a setup. The trooper was a good friend of one of our group. When he stopped by for a friendly visit, the boys saw their opportunity to give me my ration of shit and talked the trooper into playing game warden. He acted his part to perfection, and another memorable story was added to the repertoire we draw from when we are sitting around the fire and someone will slap his knee and say, "Do you remember the time when…?"

While on the subject, memory does seem to be an issue for aging anglers. A line I hear a lot these days is: "Dammit! I forgot my…."

Whether we actually forget more essential items than we did when we were younger is debatable. It just may be that our recent memory lapses are still sending up flares of embarrassment along our neural-pathways, while recollections of all the stuff we left behind during our early years is…well, forgotten. In other words, we just don't remember all the things we used to forget—if that makes any sense.

In any case, we do occasionally leave behind what we can't do without. And the oversight can prove immensely entertaining to our friends.

A good example occurred on a trip to the Tye River near Amherst, Virginia, where Bill—our retired business executive—had secured permission for Dave, me and himself to fish a section that coils through some posted land.

We loaded our gear into the back of Dave's truck and drove north out of Lynchburg on U.S. Highway 29. A few miles beyond the town of Amherst, we turned off 29 and wound our way along a tangled connection of dirt roads until we located the gate and hidden key that would give us access to the private property that adjoined the river.

We drove another half mile across some lumpy fields and parked the truck under the shade of a tall sycamore at the river's edge. We made a quick survey of the river and admired Tobacco Row Mountain profiled against the western sky before dropping the tailgate and hauling out our gear.

"OK, you two ——s, where did you hide my rod?" Bill asked. Which wasn't an altogether unreasonable question, given our common history for committing acts of that nature.

Dave and I looked at each other only briefly before knowing smiles curled the corners of our mouths. "We haven't done anything with your rod," Dave said. "Do you remember putting it in the truck?" And so the fun began.

Bill made a thorough search—there being only so many places you can hide a fishing rod in the bed of a pickup truck—before he was willing to accept that we weren't jerking him around and he really had left his rod standing in the corner of his garage. This oversight alone would have been sufficient material for creative ragging, but an added problem for Bill was a windfall for his two tormentors.

As we were pulling the rest of the gear from the truck, only two vests came out. One was Dave's; the other, mine.

"Where's your vest, Bill?" I asked. "Are you that good a fisherman that you don't need flies either?"

Bill made an emphatic gesture with one of his fingers as Dave and I continued to offer feigned sympathy and practical suggestions intended solely for our own amusement.

"If we can find some twine and a good stick, we can fix you up, Bill."

"Would it help if we put together a checklist for you? Old folks remember things better when they're written down."

This went on for several minutes as Bill endured the assault as the good sport he is. He eventually asked, "How long do you think it is going to take for me to live this one down?"

Dave's riposte was quick and deadly, like a hawk on a field mouse: "How long are you planning to live, Bill?"

Having been sidelined a time or two by a broken rod, I now carry an extra. So, after the hazing had gone on long enough, I handed Bill the extra rod and Dave supplied him with a half-dozen flies.

We all rigged up, checked our watches, and agreed to meet back at the truck in three hours. Because Bill wanted to go downriver, Dave and I agreed to fish up. The arrangement indicated no ill feeling on Bill's part. He frequently seeks more solitude in his fishing than either Dave or I, for whom three hours of silence would be a stretch. Which may or may not have something to do with why Bill seeks solitude when we three fish.

The sun was below the ridgeline and cool air was moving through the valley when Dave and I turned and headed back. We'd had a pleasant evening but brought few fish to hand, and the ones we did were dinks.

As we rounded the last bend before reaching our designated meeting place, we could see Bill standing waist-deep in a pool adjacent to the far bank, his rod bent double. Dave and I reached a spot opposite him just as he played the fish close enough to reach down and grasp it by the bottom lip. With one sweep of his arm, he hefted an eighteen-inch smallmouth high enough to be fully silhouetted against the fading light. It's bulk hung between us like a victory flag.

With a big smile smeared across his face, Bill looked at Dave and me and asked, "How did you boys do?" Sometimes justice can be a hard thing to accept.

PEE STORIES

When we were young men, we used to talk a lot about…well, you already know what young men spend a lot of time talking about. Not that we don't still talk about it; we just don't talk about it as often. Now we seem to spend more time discussing our bowels and urinary tracts. Enlarged prostates, PSA numbers, and looming colonoscopies are more frequent subjects of conversation.

Processes of elimination are important issues anytime, but especially on a fishing trip. Where one chooses to decant didn't used to be a big deal. We males had the woods mostly to ourselves—human males, anyway—and unless you happened to be particularly fastidious or excessively private, not much thought or planning was committed to where you let go. A certain amount of discretion and courtesy withstanding, of course.

But things have changed. Now our daughters are in the woods and on the streams, as well as our sons. And that is a good thing. Women fish beside us with skill and knowledge, and we expect to meet them on most any outing. We all seem to have adjusted to the new bathroom decorum this turn of events necessitates, and I haven't heard of too many problems. Although there was a transition period that did initiate a sharp learning curve for some of us.

During our camping days along the Jackson River, I emerged from my tent one morning and proceeded to release a copious stream that sent up wisps of steam as I hosed the cool, damp ground. As I was replacing the instrument of my relief, I turned around and noticed a stranger in camp who was talking to one of our group. Standing next to him was his wife.

I didn't wait for an introduction but dove for my tent, where I hid until they left, hoping they didn't get a good enough look at the top end of me to recognize my face should we happen to run into one another on the river.

Since relieving ourselves is a natural necessity that we perform often—even more now that we are past sixty—it is not surprising that a collection of memorable pee stories is part of our historical record. During our camping phase, for instance, some members of the group would take a can or bottle into the tent with them each night. The idea was to avoid having to unzip the tent flap, slip on shoes, and stumble around in the dark. You merely had to rise up out of your sleeping bag far enough to aim for the can or bottle, which would then be emptied in the morning.

Some of us were dead set against these makeshift urinals. Too risky, we averred. Besides, who wants to awaken in the middle of the night to the unmistakable sound of your sleepy-eyed tent mate urinating into a receptacle that may be mere inches from your face? Convenience or not, I could never get past the aesthetics of the arrangement.

One night the whole camp was awakened by sounds of distress and loud cursing. One of the piss-can users had upset its contents before he was able to get the lid on tight. The next day, wet sleeping bags hung in tree branches and

29

flaps were pulled back to air out the tent. It is surprising how far a little water can travel in pursuit of absorption.

Cruel jokes also occupy a place among our repertoire of memorable pee stories. One Sunday afternoon, Dave and I drove to the base of Sharp Top Mountain to fish for smallmouth in the lake near the Peaks of Otter Lodge in Bedford County, Virginia.

The area is a robust tourist destination. In addition to the lodge and lake, there are numerous hiking trails, two campgrounds, a historical building site, abundant wildlife, and a ranger station that provides planned nature activities. People are around and plentiful most anytime of the year.

Dave and I had been fishing the perimeter of the lake when I decided I couldn't ignore the urge any longer, and because no toilet was within close walking distance, I looked for a spot where I might take care of business without being seen by all the couples and families strolling by on that colorful fall afternoon.

"Dave," I said, "I'm going to duck behind that big rock and take a leak. Let me know if you see anyone coming down the trail."

Dave stood guard while I leaned my rod (fishing) against a tree, unzipped, and got things going. I was in full stream when I heard Dave's voice: "Hello, ma'am."

I drew back on the required muscles in an effort to shut off the flow. The urinary tract, I discovered, does not function quite like a mechanical faucet. The sensation felt as though an air bag had ignited inside my lower abdominal cavity. But with much tight squeezing of the buttocks and gritting of teeth, I managed to get the main valve closed and my pants zipped before I heard Dave laugh.

"Fooled you," he beamed.

You have to wonder about someone who enjoys that sort of thing.

Steve, the dermatologist in our group, also has a dramatic pee story to tell. His occurred while he was driving to the Smith River near Bassett, Virginia. The road Steve takes to the Smith passes close to Martinsville, home of the famous Martinsville Speedway. If you are not a NASCAR fan, you may not grasp the full consequences of that detail. But if you happen to be traveling near Martinsville on race day, as Steve was, you will. The traffic can back up for miles, and being stuck in traffic when you have to *really* go is everyone's nightmare.

Steve was unaware of the race when he drank several cups of coffee before setting off for the Smith. Ten miles before his turnoff, he hit the wall of traffic, just about the time the coffee kicked in.

The traffic crept. There was nowhere to pull off. And the bladder pressure mounted. At the first offramp he could access, Steve sped off the main highway and pulled onto the shoulder of the road. Exiting the car as though it were on fire, he leapt over the guardrail and landed on a three-foot blacksnake that was equally surprised by the unexpected encounter.

Steve never has cared much for snakes—a situation that has not improved since that terrified reptile coiled up his leg and hung on tight while Steve danced on one leg and hyperventilated until the two managed to detach from their mutual embrace. Steve reports that it took quite awhile for his heart rate to come down and to resume normal breathing, but in the meantime he had forgotten all about needing to pee.

Having a large, public audience for such a private affair as the one under discussion is a particularly humbling and humiliating experience. Dave and I found that out while fishing the Salmon River near Pulaski, New York.

A false salmon run takes place there each year, when the kings come in from Lake Ontario and move upriver in a futile attempt to spawn. Unfortunately for the salmon, their mating instincts are stymied by the enormous concrete power dam that blocks their passage. The salmon end up congregating in the large pool at the base of the dam, which has become a popular and overcrowded fishing spot when the fish are in.

Dave and I knew little about this fishery when we planned our trip, nor what to expect once we arrived. All we knew was that we could catch salmon there, which we can't do in our part of the country.

We got the name of a guide from someone who obviously wasn't a friend, and made arrangements to meet him on the river. It was still dark when he rowed us and his aluminum boat to the center of the collecting pool that fanned out below the lighted dam.

Having fished other rivers with other guides, Dave and I assumed that we would soon be drifting downstream. Not so. As soon as we were in the position he wanted, the guide dropped anchor. This was to be our fishing spot for the day, like fishing from a pier. Which was bad enough, but the worst was yet to come.

A few fishermen were around when we launched, but as the sun inched above the horizon whole groups began gathering, like wandering hordes of tribal warriors preparing for battle. Soon they lined the river in a shoulder-to-shoulder phalanx and began lobbing metallic lures that smacked against the water on both sides of our stationary craft.

The spectacle was astonishing. People were everywhere. Some had even taken up positions along the ramparts of the dam, which gave them a clear and unobstructed view of us in our little aluminum boat. We felt like gladiators in the Roman Colosseum.

The anxiety of being in such a conspicuous position no doubt enhanced the effects of the morning coffee. And the cold metal seats no doubt made their contribution. Whatever the reasons, Dave and I needed to empty our bladders more urgently and more frequently that terrible day than on any other day in our lives.

We battled the initial impulse until the threshold of pain made it obvious that we were going to have to face our situation…and the crowd. We aimed for discretion, but how discreet can you be when a couple hundred onlookers are so close that you can see the whites of their eyes—and the grins on their faces? For certain they saw more than the whites of our eyes. I have since wondered if we could have been cited for some offense reserved for public drunks and exhibitionists. But we were fishing, and that's different. Isn't it, your honor?

Jim, our outdoor writer, was also a victim of embarrassing public exposure. During our camping days, Dave looked up one morning to see Jim hauling butt, a shovel and toilet paper in one hand, a Playboy tucked under his arm, and the other hand barely managing to keep his drooping drawers above his knees.

He had just squatted for his morning constitutional and some light reading when a Girl Scout troop came hiking by. But that's another story about an entirely different bodily function.

JOHN GETS A NEW WIFE

John is the youngest member of our group...relatively speaking, because none of us comes even close to qualifying as *young* anymore. He had just turned fifty-seven when he found himself a brand new wife.

John had not finished with his first when she announced that she was done with him. Her disclosure was a shocker, and John took it pretty hard.

An old boyfriend whom his wife hadn't seen for decades showed up one day after his own wife died. He said he'd been advised to make contact with old friends to deal with his grief. At least that was the pretext for initiating the reacquaintance with John's then-wife.

Soon the "friendship" morphed into what was described as the ignition of a long-smoldering romance. Thus inflamed, the two old friends drove off into their retro sunset, leaving John to deal with the ashes left behind.

I don't know all the details, so I'll reign in the temptation to play judge...even though I still think John got a shitty deal.

John, who is unequivocally the gentlest soul among us, conveyed the news of his impending divorce at one of our spring gatherings. He did so with grace and dignity, and a surprising lack of animus. He put the best face on the situation and himself, but behind the equanimity and stiff upper lip, most of us could see a festering wound that told us John was still in pain.

John comes from a family of clergy whose humanitarian values are equally evident in him. His own choice of a helping profession led him to a career as a substance abuse specialist. As both counselor and administrator, he assists those addicted to drugs and alcohol in finding healthy, drug-free, and productive lives. He is the quintessential good guy, unrelentingly kind and good-natured. We all hated like hell to see him kicked and down.

But time does heal a multitude of wounds, and a year later we could see that John's spirits were arcing upward. He mentioned some women he was interested in and said he was thinking of asking them out.

We could hardly ignore such a consequential disclosure. Our buddy was thinking about dating again. A door flew open for his pals to be helpful, and we tripped over one another stepping through it.

John did not actually ask for our assistance, but we signed on anyway to share our accumulated wisdom and to advise John on how to attract a woman. We viewed his burgeoning interest in the dating scene as an opportunity to demonstrate our support and friendship. And despite what our wives may say, I am sure that our eagerness to offer counsel had nothing to do with any unacknowledged voyeurism present in a bunch of old farts who might be vicariously titillated by forthcoming episodes from John's unfolding love life.

So began our tutorial. Gathered around a campfire one evening, we declaimed on various essential subjects relative to what a man needs to do to get himself a woman, especially when the man has to rely on attributes unrelated to youth and vitality.

One of the first issues to be addressed was proper dress and grooming, an area where we all agreed John was deficient if not impaired, one that would require a large dose of our sartorial expertise.

John's choice of clothing has always stoked our curiosity. Mismatching is expected on a fishing trip when nobody really cares what you look like. But John's ingenious talent for selecting arresting apparel—such as eye-blinding colors, remnant T-shirts from the '60s, hippie sandals, floral print baggy sweat pants and such—is remarkable. And who ever heard of bringing bunny slippers on a fishing trip?

During all the years we fished together, few concerns about John's wardrobe were publicly expressed. Which is surprising, because the jumbled array of fashion he concocted begged for comment. Yet, I don't remember anyone actually saying to John's face: *What in the hell are you wearing?* We were sensitive to his feelings. Oh, there may have been some mildly chiding comment once in awhile, but I am sure it wasn't often. John seemed oblivious to the manner in which his unique dressing style contrasted with the rest of us, in any case.

But circumstances were now stirring the winds of change, and we knew strong measures would have to be taken if John were to be spared the humiliation of failed courtship. We were committed to helping, and all of us took a keen interest in the possibilities that lay before John, so to speak.

We were eager to spare him preventable faux pas—like shorts and black socks—that could short-circuit his initial pursuits of love and happiness. So it was that we embarked on a program of instructing John in the art of dressing for success.

Grooming was another unavoidable issue, given the recalcitrance of John's hair. It is a true wonder the way those tufts manage to arrange themselves in such a fascinating array of conflicting angles and curves, in the way they defy gravity, hovering in perpendicular swatches that protrude from the side of his head. Pointing out these women-deterring attributes led to a discussion of various hair lotions, shampoos, gels, creams, and conditioners. And because our orations on tonsorial decorum involved the shower, we dove into that subject, too.

Not that John needed any advice on showering: the delicate issue to be broached concerned what he does once he is *in* the shower.

Many people sing, talk to themselves, or make some form of sound while showering. John, however, is a virtuoso. Or maybe a team of virtuosos. There have been times when we wondered if he had invited a symphony orchestra to join him in the stall. So many notes and arias. Such shrieking, clunking, and banging. What decibels. Could that possibly be just one man in there? Shower etiquette was definitely on the agenda, and John absorbed an effusive outpouring of our bathroom advice.

Finally, we took up the issue of dining out. If John was going to get himself a new woman, he would inevitably end up at the dinner table, and that scene scared us all.

John is a noisy man, and not just in the shower. He is comprehensively noisy. His hearty, easy laugh could shatter glass, and the assembly of guttural eruptions, grunts, moans, and other audible tones he emits would astonish a seasoned speech pathologist. John brings all of these distinguishing traits with him to the table, and when a meal is particularly pleasing, his expressions of satisfaction rival the basal rumbling of the most satiated cattle herd gathered at the feedbox.

We drilled John hard on this issue, admonishing him that to successfully woo a woman, delicacy would need to be practiced and observed.

The campfire was burning down, and John—whose eyes were now half closed—seemed to have absorbed about all the advice he could use for the ensuing months of courtship, so we brought the suitor seminar to a close. Before dousing the flames and turning in for the night, we left John with one thought that we asked him to seriously consider. It would make a lot of sense, we told him, if he would be particularly alert to stinking-rich widows in his search for female companionship. If he were to snag such a woman, we pointed out, he might talk her into buying a trout stream that we could all enjoy. Which, as we walked off into the night, seemed a noble reason for John to find another wife.

In six months' time we were all together again. John had not only dated during the intervening months but had found someone he particularly liked who, we were to learn, was equally keen on him. Judging from his attire, which remained distinctly unaltered, and his hair, which still looked like it had been styled by a hurricane, we could only conclude that he had found his new love in defiance of all our gratuitous and wasted advice.

Throughout the five-day trip, John remained preoccupied with matters other than fishing and the company of his friends. He talked more about romance than trout.

In the evenings, he would bolt from the dinner table, cell phone in hand, and absent himself from the rest of us for long stretches of time. We would find him outside, under the stars, chatting away with a moony, teenage glow on his face. He even left early on the last day of the trip, departing like a racehorse that has just spied the barn.

Pressed for information, John unfolded his wallet and showed us a photograph of the woman who was preoccupying his thoughts and transforming his mood. Our initial response as we gathered around to inspect was stunned silence. Old John had scored, big-time. Unless the photo had been doctored, the woman was a babe.

Our interest now piqued, and lascivious male curiosity being what it is, we hectored John for full disclosure about his love life. Details, man, details. But he would have none of it. He smiled kindly, shoved his wallet in his back pocket, and he and his cell phone strolled outside.

A year later, John was a married man. His courtship with the lady in the picture had continued without our assistance or advice, and John was as happy as we had ever seen him. That was obvious from the renewed vigor that poured forth from the shower stall, as he serenaded us and all others within a hundred yards of the lodge.

Each year, at the October gathering, our group sits down to a banquet-style meal followed by a silent auction. We began the practice as a way to raise funds for some of our miscellaneous expenses. Each member brings a few items for the auction table, and all of the proceeds end up in the kitty.

One of the guys has a son-in-law who is a pharmaceutical rep. A Cialis rep, to be exact. He had given a supply of the magic elixir to his father-in-law (whether to ingratiate himself to his wife's father or at the prodding of his mother-in-law remains unknown), and several packets of the stuff ended up on the auction table.

The auction bidding is done by placing your name and offer on a sheet of paper that lies next to the desired item. An existing bid is topped by scratching out the last name on the list and adding your name with a bid that surpasses the former.

Competition for the Cialis was strong among the geezers that evening, and the column of names and bids eventually stretched to the bottom of the page. As the bidding war raged on (and this is supposed to be fun), it became apparent that John was not to be denied. He protected the list like a Prussian guard, showing little interest in any of the other items on display. And when someone scratched out John's name to place a higher bid, his pen flashed like a saber, obliterating his competitor's name and delivering a higher bid of his own.

John became increasingly more serious in pursuit of the prize. He was a man consumed by a cause. When a rottweiler gleam engulfed his face, we realized this could get nasty, and we backed off, leaving John unopposed for the coveted Cialis.

John continues to be a happy man, and we are pleased to see our friend up and in good spirits again. We also understand that his marriage is absolutely rock solid.

MOUNT COORS

Before retirement, Wayne was a CPA, a profession that placed certain restraints on the rest of us as well as him. The spring trip could never take place before the fifteenth of April.

By the time the spring trip rolled around, Wayne was ready to celebrate his release from the stresses and long hours of tax season. And he developed a remarkable reputation for his celebratory acts of gratitude and thanksgiving.

Particularly memorable was the building of Mount Coors. At the time, when we were still combining fishing with camping, Coors was the official beverage of choice, and we would lay in several cases along with the rest of our essential supplies.

April in the Southern Allegheny Mountains is not always the calendar picture of wildflowers and apple blossoms ushering in the warmth of spring. It can be cold as a freezer with flying snow. When we camped in such weather, it was customary to keep the campfire burning throughout the day. The warmth from slowly curling flames felt good on hands stiff from releasing trout into icy-cold water and bodies chilled by a late-season arctic wind. Of course, this meant that someone had to remain in camp to tend the fire while the rest of us were out fishing.

On the historic occasion for which Wayne is now revered, he—along with Ed—volunteered to remain behind. It is difficult to assess just when Ed and Wayne began reducing the stash of Coors. But it is an irrefutable fact that when the rest of us returned to camp that evening, an astonishing array of empties littered the ground in all directions.

Did they invite other campers over for fellowship? Had they thrown a party to which we had not been invited? It was a wonder to behold. It looked like the aftermath of Woodstock. Beer cans were *everywhere.*

Neither Wayne nor Ed was able to offer a coherent explanation as to what took place while the rest of us were gone, but we did determine that they had no help whatsoever in creating the remarkable landscape set before us. It was the kind of feat from which legends arise; and in this case, one did. Henceforth, the two were known among us as The Dynamic Duo.

Having received all the information we could extract from the two inebriated fire tenders, the rest of us set to work gathering up the scattered cans. The mound grew with every tinny clunk as another empty scaled its way to the top. When we were finished, we stepped back to admire the result. Someone finally broke the awe-laden silence with an observation. "Mount Coors," he declared. To which the rest of us nodded in hardy agreement.

Astonishing as it may seem, there was more to come. One member of The Dynamic Duo would add a final act to this memorable performance.

Back in those days, before we all got serious about catch and release, our group would keep a few fish to slow-cook over the open fire. After paying respects to

Mount Coors, those who had creeled fish that day carried them down to the river's edge to clean. Wayne followed along, eager to assist.

Bending over to pick up one of the lifeless trout, he pirouetted in a slow, smooth one-eighty rotation and gently settled back into the river. The water was ball-shrinking cold, but Wayne wallowed and grinned like a baby in a bathinet as the water rose above his waist. The execution of the maneuver was so delicate, so precise, that it has since been referred to as Wayne's Water Ballet.

If I had not seen so for myself, I would have questioned the claim that he regained footing under his own power and shambled, unaided, back to his tent, where he proceeded to demonstrate a fascinating rendition of changing from wet clothes to dry. For the rest of us, it was like having ringside seats at the circus.

The removal of each garment appeared as though it were being played back in slow-motion instant replay. Buttons were a particular impediment. Wayne swayed rhythmically like a willow in the breeze, his mutinous fingers stabbing at their target. He was nearly defeated in a wrestling match with his pants, and suffocation seemed imminent before he finally emerged from beneath the twisted undershirt that enveloped his head.

Success was eventually achieved, but only after a strenuous period of cross-eyed concentration and the invaluable support of a much-stressed tent pole. The results were not perfect; an errant button or two may have found their way into the wrong hole. But Wayne was once again dressed and dry. Any toddler's mother would have been impressed. Those of us who witnessed the effort broke out in spontaneous applause.

Apparently deciding that he had earned enough distinction for one day, Wayne bowed toward the tent, and rolled inside. That was the last we saw of him for the rest of the night.

In our group, Wayne has always been the first to get out of bed in the morning. Which made him the obvious choice to be our breakfast cook. We had grown accustomed to waking up to the smell of coffee and the sound of Wayne rattling pots and pans on the Coleman stove. But after the construction of Mount Coors, we all agreed that someone else would need to do breakfast the following day.

I was lying in my sleeping bag early the next morning, trying to decide if I needed to pee badly enough that I should get up or could hold off and get a little more sack time, when I heard the metallic clink of a pot lid. Raccoons, I thought, trying to get into our supplies again. Then I heard someone clear his throat, and the propane lantern flared in the darkness.

Peering through the tent flap, I could see a single figure silhouetted against the nimbus of light that spread from the lamp. Assuring myself that I really was seeing what I thought I saw, I slid down into the warm comfort of my down bag and drifted off, trailing thoughts of how reassuring it was to have a dependable accountant in our group.

When Old Fishermen Get Sick

OK, I will limit the list of maladies that legitimize our group's right to bitch and moan. But among us we can boast of high blood pressure, stiff joints, elevated blood sugar, enlarged prostates, sinusitis, back trouble, arthritis, too much bad cholesterol, and...that should do it.

We make substantial contributions to the pharmaceutical industry, and those oversize pillboxes with the separate compartments for every day of the week are standard equipment on every trip. We are poster geezers for living better through chemistry.

It is also a noticeable fact that we are twice the group we once were. Not in numbers, but in pounds. Lots of pounds.

An eight-by-ten photograph of us taken nearly twenty years ago hangs in my office. For the sake of sound mental health, I really do need to take the damn thing down. It is just *too* depressing. I hardly recognize us anymore; and I confess to resenting the smug faces on those trim young men staring back at me as I lower my bulging butt into the chair from which I write this mournful tale.

Some of us exercise, and all of us have dieted at one time or another. Currently we all claim to be "cutting back." But observing the blubber as we sidle up to the dinner table makes me wonder if the other guys might not be telling the truth about the cutting back part.

Getting older, for fishermen, is not a sissy's game. We wade more carefully. We observe greater caution stepping among the rocks. We move more deliberately. Threading a nearly invisible strand of 7X tippet through a size 22 hook takes more concentration than it used to. And in a day's time, we pull down our waders a lot more often to take a leak.

Yet, like sex, we love our fishing and hope to keep at it as long as we can. Dave jokes about having found a nursing home for us that has a trout stream flowing in front and a liquor store next door. What more could we ask for in our golden years?

Truth is, we have no reason to grumble. We still get out on the water as much as we ever did, and time has taught us a few valuable lessons. Which means we have discovered that there are a lot more gifts inside the fishing package than the size and number of fish we catch.

One is the gift of patient observance. Now, an osprey skimming the water in search of a meal, or a bright mixture of fall leaves decorating a steep canyon wall, is a welcome occasion for putting up the rod and standing motionless and attentive for a while. We have learned to appreciate all that might otherwise be missed if we were to rush through either the water or the day.

No attitude shifter is more effective than an eye-to-eye encounter with your own mortality. Fifteen years ago, George was diagnosed with colon cancer, a major killer for which the prognosis is seldom predictable.

I telephoned him at the height of his treatment and was greeted by a sluggish, halting voice at the other end. Not the typical jovial George I was used to. His words were slow and labored, signaling the heavy toll the disease and its treatment had taken. After expressing a few bromides of encouragement, I hung up, realizing that he was too ill to carry on even a brief conversation.

George's treatment regimen was taxing and continued at a snail's pace. When the next fishing trip rolled around, he was still too exhausted to attend. But after months of recovery, he turned out to be one of the fortunate. The treatment was successful, and he remains cancer-free these many years later.

We celebrated when George showed up at our group gathering, nearly a year after his initial diagnosis. He was thinner but well on the way to recovery. Yet, I sensed a change in George, one that had nothing to do with his tightened belt.

George was a storied wild-ass with a repertoire of escapades to back it up. But after his cancer, he was quieter, more reflective. I saw more intensity in his conversations around the table and the fire, and more expressed interest in the rest of us and our families. I would even say that George was a different man…and, yes, a better man as a result of all his suffering.

Such an audacious evaluation of someone else's life can only be made from a biased perspective, and to that charge I plead guilty. George and I, you see, share a bond in that we both have been humbled by the assault of a transforming illness that reminded us of the limitations of our self-sufficiency.

In the summer of 1995, a crushing episode of clinical depression obliterated any fatuous notion I might have had about being indestructible and in control. When clinical depression swarms through your body and your brain, it is possible to reach the point where finding enough energy to lift yourself out of bed in the morning becomes the major achievement of the day.

Like so many self-reliant achievers seized by depression's insidious effects, I dismissed the fatigue, donned a brave face, and carried on. The symptoms got worse, but still I refused to admit that something was wrong that I couldn't fix myself. I was the gambler at the table who has lost his stake and still doesn't have enough sense to leave the game. If I had been able, or willing, to accept the clear indicators that I was in serious trouble—and listened to those who tried to point that out—I could have spared myself a great deal of subsequent difficulty.

One afternoon as I lay on my office sofa with the door once again closed—a ruse I used to sleep while staff and colleagues thought I was hard at work—the lie I had been telling myself about pulling out of this funk on my own finally unraveled. The game was over; I admitted defeat. But enough energy remained to pick up the phone and call for help.

My perceptive physician knew immediately what was going on and prescribed a six-week leave of absence for rest and recuperation. The period of convalescence was arduous, and I experienced advances and setbacks along the way. But when I finally emerged from depression's dark tunnel, I, like George, was not the same as I had been before. Wrestling with the illness had left its indelible mark.

During my recovery, as stamina and strength returned, I spent many days on one favored trout stream or another. The soothing water invited me to slow down, to be still, to open my eyes to what is truly lasting and satisfying in a person's life.

When old fishermen get sick, we usually recover. But when we become seriously ill, we deepen our acquaintance with the fact that a time will come when we won't. During such times we contemplate the sad truth that one day there really will be one last cast. But until then, we happily string up our rods and smile at the sparkling water as it flashes by in its eternal rush to the sea.

HERETICS

If anyone should know something about heresy, it's me. Before retiring, I spent nearly forty years as an Episcopal cleric, navigating the minefields of church doctrine and canon law. I also studied church history, which included recollections of ghastly punishments meted out to the poor miscreants of antiquity who ran afoul of ecclesiastical authority.

Back in the day, you could find yourself standing in the middle of a roaring bonfire playing human marshmallow for expounding ideas that perplexed the prelates. Consider hapless Galileo. While not burned for his presumed offense, he was censured and spent the latter portion of his life under virtual house arrest. His crime? Announcing a verifiable scientific truth: that Earth rotates about the sun and is *not* the stationary center of the universe. Sad, but true.

Happily for all us argumentative types, times have changed. Deviant thinkers may still be condemned with scorching words, but burning and a stretch on the rack are off-limits.

While I formerly regarded the notion of heresy from the cool distance of intellectual objectivity, I have since come to appreciate its effects in a very personal and practical kind of way.

Our fellowship formed on the foundations of tradition. We were a group of guys who loved fishing, camping, and the out-of-doors. And one day we said, "Hey, let's make it official; let's form a club, a fishing club." And behold, it came to pass.

During the early years, everyone followed the same creed. There were no false prophets among us. We fished. We camped. Group life was cohesive. Peace and tranquility prevailed.

Then one day, a deviant desire arose in the hearts of some. The rest of us—call us the true believers—saw it as a passing whim and ignored it. How naive we were.

Antecedents to the breach date back to the day we decided to forgo camping for renting a lodge—in this case, an old, two-story farmhouse surrounded by a grassy lawn that adjoins a wider expanse of pastures and fields.

It is a beautiful place. Deer, turkey, hawks, pheasants, grouse and other wildlife appear in abundance. And the stately Allegheny Mountains stand tall in the distance. Over the years we have rented this place, some of the men have mixed in a little hunting with the fishing. Which is just fine. Likewise the horseshoe pitching. No rule breaking there.

But there are always those in a group who push the envelope of acceptable behavior and practice. One fall, Jim brought a golf bag along. If he had confined his interest to whacking a few balls into the pasture, probably nothing would have come of it. But that was not to be the extent of this intrusion into our established beliefs and customs.

One evening when Dave, John, and I returned from fishing, we were greeted by the spectacle of Jim, George, and Wayne playing a makeshift nine-hole golf course they had constructed on the lawn. Tipped-over Styrofoam cups served as holes. Which may give some idea as to just how makeshift it was.

We three fishermen shook our heads as we passed on our way to the lodge. After fixing a drink, we moved to the porch to watch and ridicule our three duffer friends… all the while wondering what was happening to our group.

Six months later, as we were unloading our vehicles for the next five-day gathering, several fully stocked golf bags appeared with the usual luggage and gear. Dave, John, and I shifted our eyes among one another as we watched the three *golfers* carry their clubs inside. In due course it was noted that while George had an impressive collection of woods and irons, not a single fly rod was seen among his stuff.

The next morning, Dave, John, and I dressed for a day on the water and laid our rods and other gear in the bed of Dave's truck. As we were putting the sandwiches and drinks in the cooler, Jim, Wayne, and George came out, pulling their clubs behind them. Each carried a pair of golf shoes, and all were dressed in brightly colored shirts and pants. They were well-attired for a day on the links.

"We have to hurry," they tossed our way as they piled into George's car. "We've reserved a tee time at the Cliffview Golf Course (an eighteen-hole course attached to a local resort)."

Dave, John, and I beheld in silence their departure from us…and our time-honored tradition. Finally, I turned to my two faithful companions and expressed what seemed to be the only appropriate response that could be made at the time: "Either of you have any matches?"

Sure Wouldn't Do That Again

A benefit bestowed on aging anglers is a backlog of memorable stories, and the leisure to contemplate the stupidity out of which some of them arose.

I would not go so far as to say longevity necessarily renders us wiser. But when we revisit an incident from our past, the perspective of time occasionally leads us to smack our foreheads and ask: What were we thinking?

Some of what we used to do was merely stupid; occasionally it was dangerous as well. I'll skip the obvious risk factors, such as driving too fast, using tobacco products, eating vein-clogging junk food, and drinking too much liquor. Mind you, we are talking about deep history here. I would not want anyone to get the idea that we might still indulge in one or more of these known hazards. Let me mention just two examples of what I know damn well my fishing buddies and I would not do again, and should not have done then, either.

In the spring of 1992, Southwestern Virginia experienced some of the worst flooding it had seen in years. Rivers escaped their banks, adjacent pastures and fields filled like reservoirs, streets morphed into streambeds, and the rooftops of low-lying houses peeked above the rising water.

Outsize clumps of soil fell from the riverbanks, carrying trees, bushes, animal carcasses, and other debris along with them. The result was a migrating mess that eventually accumulated in tangled piles wherever the current slammed against some unyielding downstream obstruction.

The heavy rains that caused all this flooding began shortly before one of our scheduled trips to the Jackson River. Because we were all still working at the time, we knew that rescheduling would be impossible. Vacation days had to be coordinated months in advance when so many calendars were involved.

For nearly a week, we followed the weather reports and talked by phone about what to do. Should we cancel? Should we go? As the departure date drew near, and we entertained the possibility of sitting at home bitching about the vagaries of nature and our personal bad luck, we decided that the trip was on.

At the time, I was living in the North Carolina Piedmont, where the heavy rains had done little more than fatten the streams and raise the level of our city's lake. All of that changed as I drove north past Martinsville and Rocky Mount and into the foothills of Southwestern Virginia.

As I turned east on Route 122, I noticed the normally languid streams I crossed were high and dark. They raced under the narrow two-lane bridges with an intensity I had never seen before. And I had been making that trip regularly for the past ten years, in every season, fair weather and foul. I was beginning to wonder just what kind of a fishing trip we were going to have…if we were to have one at all.

I met Dave at his home in Goode, where we packed his truck and drove west toward Roanoke. Later we would turn north on a series of state roads that would take us to the banks of the Jackson, where we would meet the other men.

Along the way we saw flooded lawns and places where the water stood a foot deep in the drainage ditches along the side of the road. Just twenty-five miles short of our destination, we stopped on a bridge that overlooks the Cowpasture River and watched its muddy water ripping by. The scene was not encouraging. But the rain had stopped, and we could see from the standing puddles in nearby fields that the river was slowly returning to its banks. We drove on.

When we reached our favorite campsite, we were surprised to find it above water. Just barely, as indicated by the signs of its recent submersion. Wet leaves plastered the base of tree trunks. Sticks and assorted trash dangled from the bushes. The soil was squishy damp; and the river was running just inches below the adjacent bank. But we had real estate. So we pitched our tents and set up camp.

All of us hung around camp that first day, accepting the fact that the water was too high and too fast to fish. By the next morning, breakfast behind and the whole day ahead, four of us decided to check out the river to see if we could find a place where the water was low enough and slow enough to fish some weighted flies. We stepped into our waders, strung up our rods, and started down the old logging road that led to the river.

The road—now more of an overgrown pathway from lack of use—intersects the river at a shallow-water ford... well, usually shallow. The path dips into the river at one bank, then picks up again on the opposite side.

Just downstream of the ford, a steep cliff runs along the edge of the river for a hundred yards or so. Here the river curls in a half-circle to the left, piling the water against the cliff face as it swings around the outside turn. On the inside bend, opposite the cliff, the water slows as it passes over a low, tapering bank. From where we were standing, that inside turn looked like a place where we could fish. Of course, that meant crossing the ford to get there.

Above the ford, the river pours out of a wide, slow pool. Below, it gathers speed and depth as it rounds the curve and centrifugal force drives it against the cliff. The ford is a hump in between, a saddleback that sits between the deep, slow water above and the deep, fast water below.

On most days, this is an easy place to cross. The river bottom is covered with baseball-size rocks but is otherwise flat. The water normally rolls through at knee-high depth, and during a dry season crossing can be like sloshing through a child's wading pool. But we were hardly in a dry season.

We watched a few floating sticks flash by, noting that the water was passing over the ford at a pace much faster than we were used to. And it was tainted the color of Russian tea, from all the sediment washed in by the rain. Which meant we couldn't see the bottom. But we figured we could manage. *After all, how many times had we crossed here? We know the river bottom like our bedroom floor.* Such was our reasoning, anyway.

We wanted to go about this carefully, so we decided to use sticks to help us pole our way across. This was before we started carrying fold-up wading staffs. And the enterprise we were about to undertake had a lot to do with why we started carrying them thereafter.

There were plenty of trees around, and sticks were in abundance on the forest floor. So it didn't take long for each of us to find a six-foot, sturdy branch to assist us with our passage.

With rod in one hand and stick in the other, we waded in. We immediately felt the strength of the current as it tugged at our ankles and plastered our waders tight against our shins. As we stepped forward, it pressed against our thighs like two giant hands. By the time we were a third of the way across, the water was waist-high and forcing us to lean at a steep angle on our sticks to keep from being swept away.

At midstream, the water was nearing the tops of our waders and our feet were fumbling among the rocks. We had to be particularly careful not to lift them too far off the river bottom where they might be caught by the current and put us on our faces. The only effective tactic was to proceed in a jerky, slow-motion shuffle, a few cautious inches at a time. All the while leaning hard upon our sticks.

It must have been about this point when we began to wonder if maybe this wasn't such a good idea. But no one wanted to be the first to admit it, and we were already halfway across. So we continued onward, jabbing our sticks in the river bottom, dragging our way across the angry water.

By the grace of God and the blessing of gravity, we managed to wade into shallow water and stumble onto the far bank. As we looked around at one another, the magnitude of the risk we had just taken was settling in. Had we lost our footing, the current would have swept us into the swift water along the cliff face and we would have ended up as crawfish food.

"Man, was that ever stupid," one of the guys cracked. Which amused no one, because we knew we had to cross back over to return to camp. Did he not know that?

We fished a few hours in the slack water of the river bend—even caught a few trout—before deciding that it was time to attempt the return crossing. We were extra-cautious this time, and the water seemed to have dropped an inch or two. And while it was still a butt-tightener, we made it across without incident or accident. We shuffled ashore, tossed the wading poles into the woods, and walked up the path that led to camp.

"Any luck?" asked one of the guys who had wisely stayed behind. "Yeah," I said, "we didn't drown."

Another stupid misadventure also involved water. In this case, add in ice and snow.

It was sometime in January, one winter in the late 1970s. Dave and I were both living in Bedford, Virginia, then. And we each had two small children at home.

A fierce winter storm had blown in, leaving more than a foot of snow behind. And because snow and tires are a terrifying combination for southerners, much of our civic life had come to a halt. Which typically happens whenever we get an accumulation of more than a sixteenth of an inch. But in this highly unusual circumstance, the snow was nearly two feet deep.

Schools closed, churches canceled services, stores and businesses didn't open their doors, and all meetings, gatherings, and recreational events were postponed until further notice. We were marooned for days.

Our hopes rose one afternoon when the sun appeared, its warming rays spreading a thin sheen of water across the piled-up snow. But before it could cause much melting, the sun disappeared as suddenly as it had arrived. The temperature crashed like a head-shot bird, and the slightly softened snow donned a crown of thick, hard ice. Everything was glazed: yards, trees, roads, and cars.

I still recollect the pathetic image of our cocker spaniel, Dulcinea, searching for a proper place to dump her solid waste. We would open the back door, she would climb onto the ice-capped snow, then skate recklessly on all four paws around the frozen slab.

It must have been a bewildering and humiliating experience for the poor dog. Finding no options for discreet doggy-relief, she would look toward the house with an expression of forlorn resignation, then squat on the ice sheet that once had been our yard. Before all that snow and ice melted—many weeks later—Dulcinea had dappled the encrusted surface with an expansive array of yellow Rorschachs and multiple mounds of preserved, freeze-dried poop. It was oddly decorative, dapples of yellow and brown against a gleaming background of solid white. But I suppose you would need to appreciate eccentric forms of abstract art to think so.

The bad weather went on for two years. Historical records indicate that it was more like two weeks. But when you have school-age children who have run out of patience and activities, the psychic difference between two weeks and two years can seem minimal.

Dave and I simultaneously developed a life-threatening case of cabin fever and determined by mutual pact that it would be in the best interests of all concerned for us to go fishing. Upon receiving this news, our wives were by turns incredulous—at first thinking we were joking—then concerned and irritated when they realized we were not. In a final gambit, they reminded us that the state police had issued an advisory encouraging everyone to stay off the highways unless travel was absolutely necessary, such as a medical emergency. "But Dave has four-wheel drive," we pointed out.

Dave and I listened to reason and said we understood why we shouldn't go fishing in such weather. Then he picked me up at noon.

We had decided that the James River would be our best bet. The James is wide with a steady flow, so we figured it would not freeze enough to keep us from fishing from the bank.

The quickest way to get to the James from Bedford is to take Route 43 up the mountain to the Peaks of Otter, and then drop down the other side to Buchanan. It is a steep and twisty road, especially on the backside. But as I said, Dave had four-wheel drive.

There were few cars on the road when we left, and once we started up the mountain there were none. Dave had his old S-10 Blazer in four-high, and we eased up the front side without difficulty. The same was true with the flat portion that runs along the ridge before the road breaks off again and drops down into Buchanan.

Dave and I had traveled that road many times before. There was one particular summer when we had fished the James nearly twice a week. So we knew the places where the road is so steep you feel like you are lying on your back. We were familiar with the turns that are so sharp they reverse direction. We had looked out the window and seen where the road runs so close to the edge of the mountain that you would think the car was suspended above the forest floor below…way below.

None of this would be a surprise. We knew what to expect. Besides, Dave had four-wheel drive.

The trouble began just after we dropped over the lip of the mountain and started down the backside. Because of its orientation, the sun doesn't strike that side of the mountain directly during the winter. Nor had any salt trucks or snow scrapers been that way. The road was one solid piece of slick, glittering ice.

Anticipating the steep descent, Dave drove slowly, concentrating on keeping the Blazer to the inside lane, away from where the mountain fell sharply from the road. Nevertheless, the first tap of the brake put the Blazer in a slow sideways spin.

Dave took his foot off the brake and held tight to the steering wheel until we coasted to a gradual stop. He shifted the Blazer into four-low, got us straightened out, and started down again. Slowly. Very, very slowly.

Despite the fact that we were crawling, moving no faster than one of us could walk, the steep angle of the road combined with the glossy surface provided little traction. The wheels of the Blazer slipped as much as they rolled. But we were committed. We might have been having trouble getting down the mountain, but we sure as hell couldn't turn around and go back up. So on we went. Down and down, cautiously creeping around the hairpin switchbacks. Down. Down. A few agonizing feet at a time.

I'm still somewhat ashamed to admit it, but as we approached one particularly steep and tortuous turn, I asked

Dave if it would help if I got out and walked. To make sure he didn't drive too close to the precipitous outside edge.

Dave smiled faintly, thinking I was trying to break the tension with a touch of humor. To this day, I don't think he knows I wasn't joking.

We didn't exhale until we rounded the last curve and rolled off the mountain into the center of Buchanan, a small town that rests on the south bank of the James River. On that particular day, it rested on the south bank of the *frozen* James River.

The river wasn't frozen all the way across, but it might as well have been. The ice along each bank stretched out like two silvery arms trying to engulf the dark stripe of river that ran between them.

There was no way we were going to fish from the banks. And attempting to walk out on the ice to reach the water would have been suicidal. Hypothermia sets in quickly in frigid water. Not to mention that if you fall through ice, there is always the possibility that you will find yourself in water over your head, and the ice between you and the surface.

Dave and I stared at the river for a few minutes, still basking in gratitude for having made it safely down the mountain. Although neither one of us said so, I suspect that both of us were thinking about our wives and young children and how we shouldn't press our luck with any more dumb-ass decisions.

We parked the Blazer and walked down to the river. Because we had come all that way, we thought we should at least get a closer look.

Behind a restaurant just to the right of us, we noticed a garage-door-size hole in the ice, possibly caused by some warm subsurface discharge entering the river. And it seemed to be within casting distance.

Dave and I returned to the Blazer and strung up our rods. We tied heavily weighted woolly buggers to our leaders and took turns heaving them toward the gap in the ice.

Our objective was to aim for a spot well beyond the hole. The fly would thud against the ice like a stone, then we would skitter it along the frozen surface until it plopped into the open water. We could let the fly sink only a few feet before we had to jerk it out again. If it sank any farther it would hang up on the rim of the ice when we tried to flick it out.

In between casts we picked ice out of our rod guides. The temperature was so far below freezing that water from our stripped-in line froze and clogged the guides by the time we had made but three or four casts.

We performed this fruitless exercise a couple dozen times apiece—happy that no one was watching—before deciding to call it quits. The entire procedure could not have taken more than fifteen minutes. But by then we had accomplished our purpose. By God, we had been fishing.

We took the long way home: around the mountain, through the valley in the direction of Roanoke, east toward Bedford. It was a circuitous and time-consuming way to get home. Although it probably took no longer than it did to slither down the mountain. We were able to drive the last leg on Route 460, which is fairly flat and straight. And while 460 wasn't clear of ice and snow that day, it had at least been plowed and scraped.

It was after dark before Dave and I pulled into my driveway. I was tired and glad to be home.

"So, how was it?" my wife asked.

"Oh, a lot of fun," I mumbled. "We did get to do some fishing."

Obviously picking up on my muted response, she added, "You know, that really was irresponsible."

Our children had just come into the room, and with all of us standing there together, I could hardly disagree.

SEX AND THE CLERGY

What is it about the perceptions some people have about clergy? Having been a clergyman for nearly forty years, I can attest: There are some strange attitudes out there.

Granted, some of us have brought deserved ridicule on the profession. But I still marvel at how some folks just don't know what to make of us, or what to say around us...especially when the subject is sex, or words pertaining thereto.

One summer, while on sabbatical leave, I lived in Bozeman, Montana. The purpose—at least the one stated—was study, research, and refreshment. My reason for choosing Bozeman as the venue fooled no one. Well-aware of my angling habit, the members of my North Carolina congregation had a good idea what subject I would be studying more than any other. I did make an effort to visit the library at Montana State University, but there was so much research to be done on the Madison, Yellowstone, Gallatin, Jefferson, Firehole...oh, let me not digress.

Dave, Wayne, and Ed flew out for a week to help me with my research, and I set up a float trip on the Yellowstone so everyone could participate. Because there were four of us, I contracted with a local fly-fishing shop for two boats and two guides.

We met our guides at the shop at dawn, made a short drive to the put-in spot, slid the drift boats off their trailers, and loaded our gear. Wayne and Ed got in one boat with their guide. Dave and I climbed into the other with ours.

Because of the aforementioned problem about being a member of the clergy, I typically avoid mentioning my profession on fishing trips, never knowing how strangers might react. There have been occasions when the disclosure was a mood-dampener, as though an announcement had just been made that everyone should be extra-careful and watch their mouths. It's ridiculous, but I don't exaggerate.

The salmon fly hatch happened to be in full swing on the Yellowstone that day, an event some guys plan their vacations around. The insects are so large and hatch in such abundance that the trout attack them with abandon. Being from the East, we hadn't even heard of the great Yellowstone salmon fly hatch, and here we had fallen into it by ignorance and chance. What kind of luck was that?

We were feeling giddy—catching fish, cracking jokes, and having a grand old time. Our guide added to the occasion with a series of spicy stories enriched by some equally spicy language. Not everyone can tell a good dirty joke. This guy was a master.

I have been fishing since I was five years old; I've been around some pretty crusty characters in that time and heard language bluer than the Carolina sky. I am used to it, and I hardly notice anymore. In fact, on one occasion—possibly two, but absolutely no more than three—when I have missed a good fish, an expletive has exploded from my own mouth. My buddies may tell you it has happened a lot more often than that, but knowing how they inflate stories about the fish they catch, I wouldn't consider them an accurate source.

We had a terrific morning. We were catching one fish after another, laughing at our guide's jokes, and the dreaded "What do you do for a living?" question never came up.

Around noon we drifted into a flat place along the bank to eat some lunch. The two guides carried the coolers ashore while the rest of us found a comfortable place to sit.

We ate our sandwiches and lounged on a grassy bank as we reviewed the morning's events. Ed and Wayne, both accountants, had obviously been talking shop in their boat. Just as I was about to stick a candy bar in my mouth, I heard their guide say to Dave: "Wayne and Ed tell me they are accountants. What do you and Glenn do?"

"I'm an optometrist," Dave said brightly. Turning his head slightly in my direction, he gave me a sideways glance and stretched his best here-it-comes smile across his face.

I continued to munch, knowing the trap was about to close. Dave smiled on, looking like the cat that had just eaten granny's parakeet.

"How about you, Glenn?" the guide asked, looking directly at me and my chocolate-filled mouth. "What kind of work do you do?"

"Clergy," I said. "I'm a minister, Episcopal."

Our guide—Dave's and mine, the one who had been telling all the profane stories—was rubbing his forehead when the word "clergy" brought his hand to a dead stop. His eyes shifted upward, ever so slightly. I guessed—correctly as it turned out—that he was rapidly reviewing the jokes and stories he had told over the previous few hours, and the language he had used in telling them.

The silence lasted a few seconds more, then our guide recovered—brilliantly I thought. In a voice as even and matter-of-fact as though he were telling someone the time, he said: "Well, Glenn, I sure wish you would have told me that about five fucks ago." We collapsed, laughing till it hurt.

There are those who say that story has gotten a lot of mileage, been passed around among fishing guides and their clients. I don't know about that; but I did run into a fishing guide in Virginia twenty years later who said he had heard it.

While some folks may feel the need to self-censor in the presence of clergy, that is definitely not the case with my gang. These guys cut me no slack. On a few occasions that has caused some embarrassment I would have rather done without.

Jim, our outdoor writer, has a consummate gift for ribald humor. He can turn a mundane event into a comedy routine. He is smart and witty and has a marvelous facility with pungent text. He also has a dirty mind.

Fortunately, Jim saves his most scurrilous scribblings for his friends. Which is unquestionably good for job security. More than twenty years ago, Jim began sending a written notice to all of us before the next group get-together. It started out as a fact sheet: dates, where to meet, purchases that needed to be made, who was to bring what piece of equipment—that sort of thing. But Jim is not just a writer—he is a *creative* writer. Before long, the trip notice evolved into a newsletter. Jim would describe highlights from the previous trip—grotesquely embellished—and add his unique form of editorial comment.

Truth is, the newsletter became an exhibit of adolescent male humor: lots of sexual innuendoes and raunchy rhetoric. Some would no doubt find it sophomoric. To us it was silly and fun and provided a lighthearted respite from the rigors of our professional demeanor. We all looked forward to receiving Jim's newsletter.

Jim had always sent the newsletter to my home address. But on one occasion, for reasons he has yet to explain, he mailed it to my office…the church office, that is.

I had a terrific secretary who was as proper as she was efficient. She was—as we say in the South—a fine Christian woman. She was also from the old school of secretarial training that taught her to open the boss's mail. Each day she would slit open each envelope, sort through the contents, throw away the junk, and prepare a neat, flat pile of essential correspondence for my attention.

My secretary and I occupied separate offices. On the morning we are revisiting, I had just entered hers to pick up the daily mail, a routine that included some pleasantries and a little light conversation before we both got back to work.

Trained to create a warm office atmosphere, my secretary habitually greeted all entrants to her space with cordial enthusiasm. That morning I walked into a cold-storage locker.

Her lips pursed, her eyes pinched together, she looked straight ahead. Anywhere but at me. At first, she said nothing. Most unusual, I thought. What happened to her customary cheery greeting? Had she received some bad news?

Before I had a chance to display my best pastoral empathy, she spoke. Her words frosted the already-chilly air. They came forth slowly, deliberately, the way people speak when they want to communicate through the *way* they speak, rather than through what they actually say.

Focusing on the pile of mail in front of her, she said: "There is something there from one of your fishing buddies." I had a real bad feeling about what that might mean.

I snatched the pile of mail and made a quick exit, thumbing through it as I made my way back to my own office. About midway through the stack, I found Jim's newsletter. A quick read gave me all the information I needed to figure out what could transform a warm-hearted Christian woman into an arctic glacier.

My secretary and I never spoke of the incident again, and the mood around the office soon returned to normal, except that Jim's newsletter never came to the office address again. I called him as soon as I had finished reading and told him that I would…well, I told him to never send the newsletter to the office again.

On another occasion, Jim sent a personal letter to our wives just before one of the group's scheduled fishing trips. It was a facetious piece of humor, completely tongue-in-cheek. I suppose Jim wanted the women to share in the camaraderie. That's the best I can come up with for why he did it.

He asked our partners if they might bake some cookies or prepare some other food item to send along with their husbands. He ended his request by recommending that they also give us plenty of good sex before we left to tide us over until we got back. Granted, he probably included too much unnecessary detail regarding the latter item; but as I said, Jim is a creative writer.

Most of the wives were amused, in an eye-rolling kind of way. Except one. She was definitely not amused. Now Jim doesn't send the newsletter to my office, and he definitely doesn't send any more letters to a certain wife.

While we are on the subject of sex, there was that time—back in our camping days—when we were sitting around the campfire one night, dodging the smoke and shooting the breeze. I was beat and told the boys I was going to turn in and would see them in the morning. A stifled snicker punctuated my announcement, but I thought nothing of it at the time.

I unzipped the tent and crawled inside. Leaning to one side, I rolled toward my sleeping bag…and there she was.

Lying atop the bag was a life-size, blow-up doll— flesh-colored, prone, and receptive. Her extended vinyl arms reached out to me in the darkness. Two red-capped breasts ballooned in my face, and her puffy, parted plastic thighs revealed an astonishing anatomical facsimile of a much-desired female organ.

Who in the world makes these things? And do some poor souls actually *use* them…for purposes other than playing demented pranks on their clergy friends?

The shock of discovering my bedmate was so complete I shrieked, blending my high-pitched notes with the riotous laughter taking place outside the tent. The whole caper had been carefully planned, and I still don't know how they got that air-filled hussy inside the tent without my noticing.

Now I know you have heard this before, but before we end this chapter I need to make one thing perfectly clear. And if I were standing in front of you, I would look you straight in the eyes and point my finger for emphasis: No, I did not have sex with that woman. After all, I am a clergyman.

MENTORS

Boyd was in his mid-eighties when we met. I was twenty-nine. He was a passionate outdoorsman who would soon introduce me to fly-fishing. And I sure do miss him.

Boyd has been gone for a long time, and we hadn't fished together for at least a decade when he died. But I still think of him with gratitude and affection each time I revisit the memories that have accrued since Boyd put a fly rod in my hand for the first time.

I had come to the small, rural city of Bedford, Virginia, to become the rector of St. John's Episcopal Church, where Boyd was a longtime member. This was to be my first solo assignment after a short stint as a low-ranking assistant on the staff of a congregation in Richmond. Before that, I grew up and was educated in large cities. Coming to Bedford was a change and a challenge, and Boyd helped make it one of the happiest periods of my life.

Boyd showed up at my office one morning only a few weeks after I moved in. A small, wiry man, he walked in with a slow, steady gait and looked as easygoing and comfortable as the overstuffed chair into which he lowered himself. He got right to the point as to the purpose of his visit.

"Do you like to fish?" he asked.

"Yes, I do," I replied, "but I haven't done much for years."

"Good," Boyd continued, "because you're going to need something to do besides work. When's your next day off?"

"Wednesday," I said.

"OK, how about I pick you up on Wednesday morning at eight? We can go out to my son's farm and fish his lake until lunchtime."

"Sounds good to me," I said. "I'll look forward to it."

On Wednesday morning, Boyd pulled into my driveway, and I loaded the meager tackle I had carried with me from place to place since childhood into the trunk of his car. After a short drive out of the city, we turned off the highway onto a long dirt road, at the end of which sat a spacious farmhouse owned by Boyd's son.

We parked the car near the house and hiked a few hundred yards down a long sloping field to a small lake that filled the bottomland below. I had brought along an old Mitchell 301 spinning reel and matching rod that I hadn't used in years. While digging through my old metal tackle box, trying to untangle a wad of treble-hook lures, I noticed that Boyd was stringing up a fly rod. I had seen fly rods before, but growing up I didn't know anyone who used one. I certainly hadn't.

Boyd tied a cork popping bug to the end of the leader and smoothly cast it to within inches of the lake's grassy bank. He used a wide-flexing fiberglass rod; graphite and carbon fiber rods were still several years into the future. But I noticed immediately the intimate connection between Boyd and that old fiberglass rod. Their combined movement was fluid, as though the rod were an extension of his arm. It seemed poetic to me at the time, the way the line rolled gently off the end of the rod's arching tip, launching the popping bug with just enough speed and altitude to cause it to drop with deliberate poise on its intended spot on the water.

Boyd repeated the maneuver several times, his rhythmic strokes advancing the bug a foot or so farther along the bank with each succeeding cast. I was fascinated by the display. Which grew even more dramatic when he plopped the bug next to the bank and twitched it once, and a fourteen-inch bass roiled the water as it sucked it in.

Boyd played the fish to within reach. Then reaching down, he gave the hook a quick, sharp twist, and the gratified bass turned and swam away.

"Ever use one of these?" Boyd asked, referring to his fly rod.

"No, never have," I said.

Having noticed my obvious interest, he asked if I would like to try. I wasted no time in taking him up on his offer.

Like all first-timers, I was awkward and uncoordinated with my first attempts. But Boyd was a patient teacher, and soon I grasped the concept of how the fly rod works. It would take a lot more practice before I could make a decent cast, but I had started something that would hold my interest for the rest of my life.

After that first day of fishing with Boyd—my initiation as a fly-fisher—I went out and bought a fly rod of my own. I doubt that I paid much more than twenty or twenty-five dollars for it. The year was 1975. My wife and I were starting a family, and we had little money to spare after meeting our necessities. And while I don't remember the exact amount, I do know that twenty-five bucks would have been the limit of what I could afford back then.

By all standards, the rod was a cheapie. Especially considering how much I have spent on other rods since then. But I am not going into that here. There is a chance my wife might skim through this book, and I don't want to incriminate myself by revealing any damaging information.

Nevertheless, I was pleased with my purchase and looked forward to the next time Boyd and I would fish so I could try it out. It was a thick fiberglass tube that cast like an eight-foot strand of overcooked pasta. And Boyd gave me an old Pflueger, Model 2095 reel—heavy and sturdy as a cast-iron skillet—to go with it. I was in business.

I learned to cast with that rod. I caught bass and eventually trout with that rod. I became a bona fide flyfisherman with that rod. And I fished with it until improved circumstances allowed me to afford one better.

There are wonderful memories associated with that rod. In fact, I remember that rod with as much clarity and nostalgia as I remember the first time…come to think of it, I probably better not disclose that information, either.

Boyd and I spent many Wednesday mornings fishing his son's lake, and the routine seldom varied. He would pick me up early, and we would return home by noon. At that point in his life, Boyd could no longer manage the currents and rocks of the streams and rivers he once fished. But he still had remarkable strength and endurance. In addition to the short hike to and from the lake, Boyd never sat down. From the time we arrived until the time we left, he fished.

Boyd was my fly-fishing mentor throughout the five and a half years I lived in Bedford. And despite the notable difference in our ages, we became regular fishing buddies.

He introduced me to the sport, taught me to love it, and passed along a now-cherished collection of memorable stories. Such as the one he repeatedly told about the monster bass he used to catch on his trips to Currituck Sound—back in the days when there were monster bass in Currituck Sound to catch. He also imparted sage advice on the philosophy of why we fish.

When I started fishing with Boyd, I was hell-bent on catching as many fish as possible and counting every one. Boyd interrupted one of those fish-counting frenzies once by asking me if I had noticed how vivid the fall colors were that day, then quickly segueing into a reminiscence of the good people he had fished with, and all the rivers and streams he had known. Then he paused and said, "You know, if I never catch another fish, I've caught my share." It would be a long time before the wisdom of those words sunk in. I wasn't capable of appreciating them at the time, and I suspect Boyd knew that but dropped them like seeds he hoped would one day grow.

In 1981, I left Bedford to become the rector of a larger church, with more responsibility, in another state. I never saw Boyd again. He continued to fish for several years after I left. But eventually he became feeble and had to put down his fly rod for good and move to a skilled-care facility. I can only imagine how difficult that must have been for him. Then one day a friend informed me that Boyd had died. I often think of him, as I do now with a lump in my throat, but never more than when I pick up that old Pflueger reel, the one that has been so durable and so dependable for all these years.

While Boyd was the mentor who turned me into a fly-fisher, he was not the one who first taught me how to fish. That distinction belongs to my paternal grandfather.

My grandfather was mostly a bait fisherman. Although, he would occasionally use a Dardevle spinnie or one of his balsa-wood lures with dual sets of treble hooks dangling from their undersides. He was an effective fisherman but cared nothing about finesse. For him, catching fish was the purpose of the sport, and what he caught he kept. If that meant using an impaled worm that hung below a golf-ball-size bobber, or a brace of tail-hooked minnows, that is what he did. Whatever it took to get the job done. I doubt that catch and release would have made any sense to him.

From the time he was a young man, my grandfather worked in the steel mills of Pittsburgh. It was a hard life, and fishing was his main recreational release.

Those were the days before anyone worried much about air quality, and the EPA hadn't even been thought of yet. In addition—like so many men of his age and class—he had a cigarette in his mouth for most of his waking hours.

He was eventually diagnosed with emphysema and had to retire early. Nevertheless, he continued to smoke, and his health worsened. Yet he still fished, even when he could hardly draw his breath.

My daughter has a framed newspaper picture of my grandfather that hangs in her dining room. The photograph was taken shortly before he died. He looks skeletal. A rumpled, wide-brimmed hat droops over his hollow face, making it look even more shrunken than it is. His shirt and pants hang from his frail limbs, the way they would on any garden scarecrow. In his right hand, he lifts a stringer with two rainbow trout tethered to the end. He is smiling. He is only 62. In a few months, he will be as dead as the trout he holds.

During the last two years of his life, my grandfather frequented a pay-to-fish lake a few miles from his home. It was stocked, and bait could be purchased at the snack bar.

Grandfather would drive out to the lake, and because he had permission from the owner, park his Pontiac Ventura next to the water. He would retrieve a fold-up lawn chair from the trunk, along with his tackle. Then he would bait up and sit in that chair by the hour, waiting for the white bobber to go under, signaling that one of those stupid stocked trout had just ingested one of the night crawlers that were sold in Styrofoam cups.

Occasionally, during those last couple of years before his lungs completely gave out, my grandfather would take me with him when he fished. I was ten, eleven years old, with the energy of a nuclear plant and the attention span of a horsefly. While he sat in his chair waiting for a bite, I would thread pieces of cut-up worms onto small hooks and catch bream by the bucketful.

Grandfather was a quiet man, a notably poor conversationalist. But whether through words exchanged or more likely the intuition that children have, I knew my grandfather loved me. And I loved him.

A few items from my grandfather's tackle box are displayed on a shelf in my den: three dinged-up lures, one plastic hook keeper, a pocketknife, one tip-up bobber, and his Zebco 33. That is about all I have left of him, except for the memories and that picture from the *Pittsburgh Post-Gazette.*

There is a reason I gave that picture to my daughter, and believe me, it was hard to give it up. For years it hung in my own house. But I had an agenda for passing it along. You see, I now have a grandson of my own, young James, who is barely two years old. I want James to grow up with the picture in his house, because I hope that one day he will ask about the frail old man holding up two trout. It may have been a shameless act, but I wanted to plant some ideas in his head.

Since I am into this confession, I might as well go ahead and tell it all: I also gave my daughter a framed print of a gray-haired old man and a young boy to put in James' room. The perspective of the picture is from the rear, as though the old man and the boy are walking away from the viewer, toward an unseen destination.

The boy is small and reaches up to hold the old man's hand. They are both carrying fishing poles and wearing vests. A tackle box is in the old man's other hand. There is little doubt where the two are going.

On a recent visit to my daughter's home, I was in my grandson's room, helping to get him ready for bed. I had just read him a few children's stories and was lifting him in my arms when he pointed to the picture, which sits atop his chest of drawers. He put one of his small arms around my neck, hugged me, and said: "Grandpa and James."

"Absolutely," I said, hugging him back, "Grandpa and James."

"And Boyd and grandfather," I whispered to myself. "Fishing buddies all."

TOUGH GUYS

There's this guy I met at a social gathering—he is around my age—who used to play some kind of contact sport. We were chatting over a drink when he started telling me how rough it was, insinuating he was a real tough guy, I assumed.

It really annoys me when old guys brag about the glory days. "Listen," I said, "if you think your sport was rough, you should have been a flyfisherman."

I started telling him about the cuts, bruises, and scratches we flyfishermen get from crashing on slippery rocks or falling down steep, rocky slopes, and the lacerations we endure from squirming through barbed wire fence.

To be specific, I told him about the time Dave was working the bank of a fast-moving stream, tripped, and started to fall backward into the water. Executing an acrobatic twist, he reached toward the bank to grab a handful of branches that turned out to be briers.

The maneuver broke his fall. But as his hands slid down the length of the vines, they stripped them clean, depositing large, nasty thorns in the flesh of his palms. Jim was nearby and saw the whole bloody thing. He said Dave could have auditioned for the circus—as the strange hybrid-man with porcupine hands.

I also considered telling the guy about the time Ed fell out of a tree with such an earth-shaking thud we were sure he'd been injured. He wasn't, to everyone's astonishment. But since alcohol was involved in that story, I thought better of it.

Instead, I told him about chigger bites, poison ivy, stinging nettles, and ticks. I described yellow jackets, mosquitoes, and other venomous pests we avoided by dousing ourselves in substances now banned by the EPA.

In my haste to set the record straight, I nearly forgot to mention snakes: the copperhead that decided to join Dave and Bill and me in our campsite, and that surprised reptile (nonpoisonous, thankfully) I inadvertently grabbed while climbing over a large rock on a high-gradient mountain stream.

Then I asked the guy if he had ever been threatened by feral dogs on *his* playing field, as we fishermen have been on ours. And if he thought a two-hundred-pound linebacker was intimidating, I advised him he should try being chased by an angry bull, as Dave and I were when we crossed an open pasture en route to the James River.

I followed that story with the one about the beaver that attacked Dave—surfacing and circling like a furry rendition of Jaws, Dave whacking at it with his rod and keeping it at bay as he slowly backed up and retreated from the pool.

The last animal encounter I described was the one about the raccoon that ambled into camp during the middle of the day when Bill, Dave, and I were camped on the Shaver's Fork near Cheat Mountain, West Virginia. The critter's unnatural behavior gave us reason to believe it might possibly be rabid. But, thanks to Bill, it passed away suddenly from an acute case of lead poisoning, giving us no further cause for concern.

As the conversation went on, it was obvious this bragging old athlete needed to be reminded that there are specified safety rules for the protection of players in his sport. Not so in fly-fishing. I informed him that my buddies and I have wet-waded all day in water that was downstream from noted polluters. And the only safety warning we ever got was an advisory against eating the fish: Doing so could endanger your health.

And speaking of health, Steve is the dermatologist in our group. He has put the fear of God in us about wearing sunscreen, and we do. But his sound medical advice came too late for our group. Most of us had already spent so much unprotected time fishing in full sun, before we knew any better, that we have to make regular appointments to have suspicious lesions removed from our skin. Steve also claims that one of his medical journals has reported on a new orthopedic syndrome: fly tier's finger. According to the report, a 50-year-old male lawyer was diagnosed with "leukonychia of the left index finger," which his doctor attributed to the fact that the man spent "a minimum of four hours a day mounting and designing his own flies."

Steve is a good man to have along on fishing trips. He brings potions and remedies for all sorts of mild discomforts, such as the carpal tunnel symptoms I was having after casting a heavy rod from daylight to sunset while on a trip to Alaska. Steve can also perform light field surgery in an emergency, such as the time we asked a mutual acquaintance to join us on a trip to the Smith River in Virginia. The man had just taken up fly-fishing and hardly knew the first thing about casting a line. He was also hardheaded about taking any advice from either of us; so we left him to his own instruction and went off to fish another part of the river.

It was a gusty day, which made casting tricky for even the most experienced angler. After an hour or so, we saw our guest walking briskly toward us with a #8 woolly bugger attached to his neck, right next to his Adam's apple. When he got close enough to speak, he told us how he had tried to force a cast into the wind and hooked himself. Each syllable he voiced, each rise and fall of his Adam's apple, made that woolly bugger dance on his neck like it was trying to crawl away.

It was hard to refrain from laughing at the man's misfortune. Which, I am ashamed to report, we didn't... refrain from laughing, that is. Steve did extract the hook with commendable skill, but the man never has fished with us again.

Jimmy has the rare distinction in our group of having visited the emergency room twice in one day for hook impalement. When he made the return visit—only hours after the first—to have the second hook removed, the attending physician noted that it was deja vu all over again.

The bragging erstwhile athlete was about to interrupt me when I reminded him of the possibility of drowning that all fly-fishers face. Nobody in our group has come close to that; but it does happen.

Other than Steve and I being surprised by an unexpected and unannounced water release while fishing below a hydro dam, which forced us to do some haul-ass scrambling to get to the bank, the worst that has happened to our group has been a rare canoe dumping, or the occasional dunking from tripping over a rock or stepping in a hole. Although, filling up your waders can be like standing naked in a meat locker if the water happens to be frigid and the wind is blowing cold.

Dave and I made an early spring trip to the Catskills a few years ago. In fact, we went too early. The water temperature was so low the fish and insects were still vacationing in Miami and were nowhere to be seen. I've handled ice cubes warmer than that water. I know because I fell in: a complete full-body immersion.

As I came up for air, hyperventilating from the shock of the icy water, I stumbled and went down again. Dave, who was standing nearby, still says it was the most entertaining moment of the trip. He particularly likes to tell the part about how the only piece of me he could see was my hat floating on the surface.

The more I think about what Dave finds entertaining, the more concerned I become. For instance, there was that time in Bozeman, Montana, when Wayne had an allergic food reaction, and we drove him to the hospital in the middle of the night. As the doctor led Wayne to a curtained cubicle, Dave called after him: "Wayne, if you don't make it, can I have your traveler's checks?"

Dave did get his comeuppance one afternoon while fishing a friend's lake for largemouth bass. He was encouraged to wade out a few feet from the bank for a better casting position. It was a setup. Unaware of the ledge he was on, he stepped off the end and had to swim for shore. It was a most enjoyable performance for those fortunate enough to have been present.

Oh, and I did remember to tell the man I was listening to about the time Steve found himself stranded on a rock ledge in the middle of the Stillwater River in Montana, with deep water all around. How he got in that position is too long a story to go into here. It was his good fortune that a cowboy happened by (seriously), saw Steve's predicament, and threw him a rope; then he proceeded to haul him across the water like a human water ski. Steve might not admit to that incident, but in a regrettable moment of self-disclosure he confessed it to me, and I really do believe it should be shared.

At this point in the conversation, I paused to sip my drink. I was beginning to tire of this guy going on about himself and all his on-field exploits. But I caught my breath and moved on. There were a couple more things he needed to hear about the manly sport of fly-fishing.

While no one in our group has ever gotten lost in the woods, I wanted my conversation partner to know about the disoriented fisherman who did while searching for a remote little stream in a rugged section of the Blue Ridge Mountains. He ended up spending the night on the ground before finding his way out the following day. It was not a pleasant experience.

Neither was the one that occurred to a fellow angler we know who stepped on a subsurface log that rolled and pinned his foot to the streambed. He carved on the log with his penknife—which took quite some time—until he was able to free his foot and limp back to the car on his damaged limb.

I also told about the time Dave and I were walking the tracks through a deep gorge and a freight train overtook us. The man needed to know that there is no sudden-death tiebreaker nearly as exciting as being plastered against a vertical embankment while two hundred deafening coal cars screech past your nose.

Much the same thing, I advised him, can be said about lightning. Fly-fishers are frequently chased off the water when the sky gets electrical; but I'll never forget the time a megaton bolt struck just as I started crossing a very rocky section of the Greenbrier River in West Virginia. My companions acknowledge that there is a record of someone having done so previously, but it was the first time any of them had ever seen a man walk on water... or, rather, run.

It was time to wrap up this conversation, and, wanting to be brief, I concluded my defense of fly-fishing's rigors with an illustration of its mental and emotional demands. The one that came to mind was the afternoon I was fishing the Jackson River, in Virginia, dressed in my finest sporting attire, which included an expensive Irish wool sweater I had received for Christmas. Any outdoor catalog would have been pleased to have me on its cover.

Several scruffy good old boys were on the bank, dunking worms and watching as I cast flies...and a fashionable angler image. It was near midstream that I fell. It wasn't a bad fall, just enough to create thrashing and make that elegant wool sweater look as though I were tangled in a giant wet mop.

Not a word was said by any of the good old boys, either when I fell or when I crawled up the bank, dripping like a faucet. They just continued fishing, as though nothing had happened.

The silence continued as I set off down the path toward camp. Then, as I turned a corner and was out of sight, I heard a spontaneous explosion of howling laughter.

Believe me, it takes a lot of mental concentration to keep something like that from interfering with your game.

With that having been said, I downed the last of my drink and walked off. I had heard enough, and you know how annoying it is to listen to old guys tell of their adventures and brag about the glory days. You know what I mean?

WINTER RIVER: A POETIC INTERLUDE

During the steely-cold days of winter, when each new arctic assault urges us closer to the hearth, the rivers that flow through our warmer days are neglected and all but forgotten. But not by me.

"Why do you go there in this weather?" friends ask. "To fish," I say, as I grab my fly rod and pull the woolen cap down over my ears. I can tell by their faces they don't believe me...then neither do I.

Leaving the car at the side of the road, I trudge through the wide pasture that leads to the water's edge. The ground is rock-hard, and frozen grass crunches under my boots. Last fall, grasshoppers would have scattered like popcorn in front of me with each planted step, but today they are nowhere to be seen—nor are the chirping crickets, the busy ants, or the sluggish black beetles that are gobbled by the trout when they lose their way and fall upon the water.

As I get closer to the river, a scene cast in browns and grays awaits me. Gone are the green leaves of summer and the rainbow hues of autumn. It is a picture of bark and earth I see. There are no wildflowers twinkling in the shadows, no purple berries dangling from the briers that tore my waders one evening last June. Even the greedy kudzu patch looks deceptively satisfied, its long barren tentacles hanging peacefully from trees they long ago enslaved.

With the exception of a few parched remnants of fall foliage, the deciduous trees are empty and bare. In summer they seemed to merge into leafy togetherness; but now they stand alone along the river's edge, their naked branches entwined, as though clinging to one another in the face of the harsh winter wind.

Looking up, I see a majestic chunk of the Blue Ridge Mountains that forms a backdrop for the river. Stripped of its canopy, the mountain is dark against the cloud-laden sky. Jagged rocks, formerly concealed, are now revealed; and I see acres more of the drab forest floor. Even the now-flowerless rhododendrons have faded into the bleakness, and only the sparsely scattered cedars and a few scruffy pines interrupt the dull and somber tones.

Without its warm-weather clothes, the mountain is immodestly exposed: Each bulge and depression is more prominent, each contour more angular, each peak and valley more sharply defined. The mountain, too, is a cold, austere sight that befits the season and the day.

I string up my fly rod and prepare to fish, as snow begins to fall. The breeze has stilled, and large, wet flakes descend gently through the air. I tuck the rod under my arm and watch as they enfold the outstretched branches and cover the ground beneath. The bright snow sticks to everything...except the river, which cuts a dark, winding gash through this sparkling world of white. It is a wondrous sight, as though the earth has drawn a soft, linen blanket around itself to await winter's end.

There is a deep stillness in the air, like a held breath, full of anticipation. Everything is quiet, except for the river, which continues on like a giant artery winding in and out of the seasons. It is the one constant in this frozen scene around me. It is the touchstone of memories, the sole herald of spring. It is the bearer of promise that comes from deep within the resting earth.

When I return home, I know what friends will do. They will shake their heads, stare with incredulous eyes, and ask me again why I come here.

To fish, I will say. Why else would I go to the river in winter?

Two Frights in Alaska

It's an inauspicious way to begin, I know, but I have to say upfront that I can't disclose the identities of my two buddies who feature in this story. A portion of what follows contains—as a broadcaster would be required to intone—graphic material that some may find offensive.

So I won't use their names; I'll protect them. Which is really too bad because they deserve to be recognized, or exposed, whichever the case may be. Truth is, I don't want them to sue me in the event their wives find out. More on that later, but first…Alaska!

As soon as we got off the plane at Anchorage International Airport, I knew we were in wild country. All around, sports like us were picking up their gear: bloated canvas duffel bags and well-worn backpacks trimmed out for a backcountry trek. This definitely was not the scene I was used to when I stake out a position at the baggage carousel.

There wasn't a suit in the crowd. Some of the hunters who had flown in were already dressed in camouflage clothes and waterproof boots. Along with their bags, they were collecting rifles and bows, which they had packed in sturdy metal boxes or hard plastic cases with locks on the lids.

Meanwhile, the fishermen—which included our group—were corralling their fly rod tubes.

We fishermen were definitely in the majority. I doubt that the number of briefcases coming off a commuter out of New York City could have surpassed the number of fly rods I saw.

This was the first trip to Alaska for all but one in our group, and we were as aroused as deer in rut at the prospect of hooking up with some of the outsize rainbows we had been hearing about. But it had been a long day of flying since leaving Piedmont Triad International Airport in Greensboro, North Carolina, earlier that morning, and the first thing we had to do was check into our hotel and get some sleep.

The next day, we flew on small aircraft deeper into the Alaska backcountry, where we would spend the week at a full-service fishing lodge that caters to anglers from around the world. The lodge was equipped with seasoned guides, a fleet of jet boats, and three small aircraft—including two float planes. With such resources at our disposal, we would cover long distances and fish where the fishing was at its best.

Each morning we would arise before six, eat a big breakfast, and board either a jet boat or a float plane to reach our daily destination. We fished all day, stopping only to eat a multi-course shore lunch cooked on an open fire by our versatile guides, who were as adept at outdoor cookery as they were at locating fish. And such fish. They were large, muscular, and as wild as the environment in which they were caught.

Before proceeding further, I realize I have used "wild" at least twice already. And, yes, dear reader, I am aware of your intolerance of redundancy and—worse—clichés. But I beg your patience, as I believe it to be the precise and perfect word for introducing two frights I had that week—frights that only a place as *wild* as Alaska could provide.

The first fright occurred around midmorning on the fourth day. Two of us, along with our guide, left the lodge by jet boat to travel up the Tazimina River in search of some of those hefty Alaska rainbow trout. A jet boat, in the event you are unfamiliar, is a large johnboat with a jet outboard engine attached. It is a highly maneuverable craft, perfect for jetting upstream in a strong, boulder-strewn river that would easily shear the propeller off a conventional outboard motor.

We had traveled a mile or so upriver when our guide pulled into some slack water and told me to step out and start fishing. He said he was going to drop my buddy off at another promising spot downstream and would be back to check on me later. With that, he roared off in a spray of foam.

I watched the boat juke among the rocks, then lean hard to the left and disappear around a bend in the river. I was alone, with no guide or companion.

Because I didn't know this river, I proceeded cautiously: staying close to the bank, out of the heavy current, wading with extra care and concentration. When I reached a place where the current curved in and ran along the bank, I climbed out and walked through the woods that bordered the river's edge until I found a safe spot to reenter.

It was there I began to notice that uncomfortable sensation you get when you sense someone is watching you. I didn't see anyone or any *thing* unusual. Nor did I hear anything out of the ordinary. But our senses do seem to develop heightened awareness when we are in unfamiliar surroundings. My guess is it has something to do with our primordial instincts for survival. And something was clearly spooking me.

For no apparent reason, I felt a tingle at the base of my spine as I stepped off the bank. My head rotated about a half turn as I slipped into the river, and the tingle ramped up to a full-spinal alert.

I saw it just as it saw me. Our heads came up in unison and stopped when our eyes met. There was eye contact. Believe me, there definitely was eye contact. I won't ever forget those eyes.

The bear had been busy eating salmon that had washed up on the bank; and either because I had been downwind of it or because it was distracted by the salmon dinner, it was obvious that the bear was as surprised as I was.

Our encounter could not have lasted more than a few seconds, but some seconds sure do seem a lot longer than others. These must have lasted at least ten minutes each, or so it seemed.

It astonishes me now, when I consider all I was able to think about in so short a time. Don't tell me the human brain isn't as quick as a computer. I was a human high-speed processor during that moment. How else could I have recalled everything I had ever read about bear encounters; determined the best climbing branches within fifty yards; calculated how fast the current would carry me away if I jumped; examined all signals that would indicate the bear's level of aggression; reviewed my life up until that point; asked forgiveness; and wondered what people would say at my funeral. All within three or four seconds!

After our eyes locked, the bear rose up on its hind feet, brandishing flesh-eating fangs at least a foot in length. Its head was the size of a refrigerator, its claws as sharp as razor wire. This was so large and fierce a bear that even King Kong would have been intimidated. No bear in Alaska has ever been bigger, meaner, or more fearsome.

Well, that is how it seemed at the time, anyway. The truth is, this amiable, average-size bear didn't want any more to do with me than I did with him. He gave me the once-over, sniffed the air with indignation, and shambled off into the woods. I checked my shorts and waited for the guide to return. I'd had enough solitary fishing for a while.

The second fright didn't occur in the vast Alaska wilderness, but in the wilds of the city of Anchorage. And as I was to discover, there are some pretty wild places to be found there, if you know where to look, which my so-called fishing buddies clearly did.

On one of our nights in Anchorage, two of my buddies told me they wanted to take me to a special place for dinner. One of them had made previous trips to Alaska and said he had been there before and highly recommended it. His vague description told through a muted smile made me a little suspicious, but I let it pass.

The cab picked us up at the hotel, and the guy with the previous experience mumbled our destination to the driver. As soon as the cab pulled up, I knew this was no restaurant. Oh, you can purchase food there; my buddies didn't misspeak about that. But food wasn't the purpose of this establishment.

Pulsating music spilled out of the entryway, and a partially dressed woman waited to greet us at the entrance. While I am no expert here, I believe the term most often used to describe such places is "Gentleman's Club."

One of the guys paid the cabby and, along with the other member of our trio, made a beeline for the door. What was I to do?

That tingling sensation at the end of my spine reappeared as soon as we stepped inside. This time it wasn't because of something I sensed might be watching *me*, but because of what I was seeing through my own two eyes—which must have been the size of baseballs at that point.

Alternating colored lights from somewhere overhead swept through the dimly lighted room. The music was loud. In the center was a stage with tables all around, at which sat groups of men sipping drinks and sucking on long-neck bottles of beer.

At the edge of the stage, two women undulated to the beat of some heavy-metal tune that hadn't assaulted my ears since the days when my children were living at home. It was a wild piece—oh, there's that word again—and these two women were really into it.

By the time we showed up, most of what they had been wearing lay scattered on the stage. The only garment remaining on each of them was a narrow patch of cloth between their legs, precariously attached by the tiniest bits of string…not that I was looking all that closely.

In any event, those, too, hit the floor before we made it to our seats.

The next time I looked, the two women were performing a lower-body gymnastic routine. And despite my earlier disclaimer, there is just so much detail I am willing to offer here. Let it suffice to say that their demonstration would have been an excellent visual aid in a medical school classroom: Something like Introduction to Gynecology comes to mind. And the guys perched around the stage were having no trouble concentrating on the lesson.

For all of my working life I had been a cleric. This was a novel situation—a delicate one, too. And it was about to get more delicate.

After we found a table, my two buddies went off to get some drinks and snacks—the dinner I was promised—leaving me alone to fend for myself. Shortly after they departed, the tingle in my spine that had ensued when I came in suddenly got urgent (life-threatening may be more accurate) when I looked up and saw her coming.

No, she can't be, I thought. *Why would she be coming over here?*

I shielded my eyes with one hand and tucked my head between my shoulders, turtle-style, hoping to avoid detection. It did not work.

The first thing I saw were the stiletto heels at the end of her naked legs. Pretty nice legs, too…pardon me, I digress. Slowly, I lifted my head and peeked between my fingers. Our eyes met. "Want a lap dance?" she asked.

I am a fast learner, and in the short time I had been sitting at the table, taking in all the activity around me, I had already figured out what a lap dance was.

What was a happily married cleric on a vacation fishing trip to do? And another thing, nobody better ever try to one-up me when it comes to sharing stories about awkward moments.

"I just got here," I replied…or, rather, stammered. It was the best I could come up with at the time.

The woman, probably noticing that the blood had drained from my face, must have figured that even if I said yes, she might have a cardiac arrest on her hands.

"Maybe later," she said with a smile. Then turned and walked away, twitching that magnificent —. Sorry, I was about to digress again.

By the time my friends got back with the drinks and snacks, I concluded that I had done sufficient missionary work for the evening. I had come to Alaska to be exposed to adventure and new experiences, but a body can only endure so much exposure at one time.

I told my two friends that I needed to leave and went outside to hail a cab. As I was heading back to the hotel, I was thinking about making another trip to Alaska. And when I do, I don't want to be surprised by the bear…or the bare, for that matter.

MISFITS

Steve and I had been friends and fishing buddies for nearly thirty years. During that time, we saw a lot of each other: fishing, traveling, socializing with family and friends. Then we had to say goodbye.

In the spring of 2008, I retired from my position as rector of St. Mary's Episcopal Church in High Point, North Carolina. I had practiced ministry there for more than twenty-seven years, and been an ordained Episcopal cleric for nearly thirty-eight. I had turned sixty-two the previous November, and my wife, Kathy, and I decided we needed more time for each other and our first grand-child, who had arrived the previous spring. More fishing may have figured in the calculation, too.

Evidence-based studies—supported by an array of anecdotal horror stories—make it clear that a new pastor has difficulty getting established with a congregation when the old guy hangs around like a musty odor that won't go away. I suppose those of us who fall into that category mean well, but too often we get in the way because we can't let go. That circumstance, along with the desire for another adventure before we were too old for adventures, convinced Kathy and me that we should sell our house in High Point and move back to Virginia. It proved to be an exhilarating decision, but not without some grief and loss. Which brings me back to Steve.

I met Steve several months after I arrived in High Point. He had come to town a year earlier to begin his medical practice, having just completed a residency in dermatology. I needed a skin doc; he was recommended. That is how it all began.

During the get-to-know-you chitchat that precedes an initial doctor/patient consultation, we discovered that we both liked to fly-fish. We also noted that neither of us had explored many of North Carolina's rivers and streams, mainly because we hadn't found a buddy to do it with. Within a week, we were waist-deep in water, casting flies to trout on what would be the first of many rivers we would wade together over the next three decades.

We got to know the local water well, and as the years passed we broadened our range to include trips to Maine, Pennsylvania, Montana, Alaska, and Wyoming. One year, Steve asked me to come along on his annual fishing trip to Canada with his brothers—a trip they had been making since they all were in their teens.

Our destination was a fish camp on a small island in the middle of Lady Evelyn Lake. Lady Evelyn is a vast and meandering body of water, which meant we some-times had to travel over water for as much as an hour to find the best fishing. This we did in small, cedar-strip boats, powered by fifteen-horsepower outboard motors.

Steve and I were fishing together early one afternoon when a few storm clouds began congregating in the west-ern sky. Because they didn't seem to pose a threat, we fished on. However, there is an old saying about Canadian weather we should have heeded: If you don't like it, stick around for an hour; it will change. And change it did.

Those non-threatening clouds called in reinforcements, and before we noticed what was happening, they charged. As the first sheets of rain attacked, Steve and I secured our rods and fired up the outboard.

Rain fell in such abundance we could see only a few yards ahead. Then a muscular wind arrived, whipping up whitecaps that hammered the sides of our little wooden boat.

Steve is by nature a calm and even-tempered man. Seldom flustered, he responds to the most agitating experiences with cool equanimity. He also has an encyclopedic mind, the kind of mind that retains all sorts of trivial details. Which is a good thing when you have to remember a lot of diseases and pharmaceutical remedies. But it is definitely *not* a good thing when you are in the midst of a maelstrom that might dump you into an ice-cold lake and your fishing buddy is not as unexcitable as you are.

As we rocked and bounced over the wind-driven waves, Steve reported—in his best bedside-manner voice—his estimate as to how long it would take for hypothermia to overcome us in the event we ended up in the water. Which at that moment seemed like more than a hypothetical possibility. That really was information I could have done without.

Despite the scare, our little boat kept us afloat until we reached a small island where we came ashore and waited out the storm. Which passed in true Canadian fashion. In about an hour, the sun reappeared and we were fishing again. So ended an adventure that would be one of many as the years passed and our friendship deepened.

Steve and I were a natural fit, with far more in common than just the fishing. For one thing, we both read a lot of books. Which gave us plenty to talk about during those long drives to and from the streams. We would drive, often for hours, with seldom a moment's silence. We would discuss literature, education, politics, science, religion... and solve a large portion of the major issues facing western civilization during our time in history.

We also had a fondness for food served in small country restaurants, those mom-and-pop places where you know the food is good because of all the cop cars pulled up outside. Law enforcement officers, who spend so much time behind the wheel, always seem to know the best and cheapest places to eat.

Steve and I made a habit of stopping at such places and had some designated favorites along our regular routes. There was one in eastern Tennessee—nearly hidden behind a small mountain of old tires belonging to the dealership next door—where we could get a large bowl of pinto beans, a slab of corn bread, and a drink for less than two dollars.

The building was nothing more than a cinder block square, about the size of a high school classroom. Inside, no visible effort had been mounted to create what other eateries might call atmosphere. The surroundings made one clear statement: This is a place for eating, nothing more.

On our first visit, we stood in line to order from a handwritten menu. And when our order came up, we carried it ourselves to one of the Formica-topped tables that lined the walls and formed one neat row down the middle of the room. Around those tables sat farmers and other working folk who filed in and out on their lunch hours, and who kept those tables full. After our first bowl of pintos, we were hooked.

There was still more that Steve and I had in common. We exercised at the same YMCA. We gardened. We enjoyed plays and lectures. We had some of the same friends. But most important of all, we had similar backgrounds, backgrounds that stood out in the old southern city to which we had come to live and work.

It's not that the good folks of High Point were unfriendly. They were anything but. After all, they were mostly Southerners. But Steve and I had a different kind of growing up from most of the people we knew, and the disparity misaligned the edges of a good tight fit. At least it felt that way to us.

Now I don't want to make too much of this, but if you are not from the south, or have never lived in the south, you may be clueless about some of the still-functioning norms that govern genteel southern living. Trust me, such attributes as genealogy, heritage, legacy, and long-standing family connections still matter.

Shortly before Steve completed his residency in dermatology, he interviewed several practices while searching for a place to begin his medical career. In one large Virginia city, he was wined and dined by a prestigious group of doctors and their wives. During the dinner, he was asked by one of the wives if he was an FFV (First Families of Virginia). Steve had to ask the woman what she meant. Which must have been all the information needed to size him up. The interview, Steve said, went downhill from there.

After Steve told me his story, I told him one of mine, which took place in Richmond, Virginia. While I was sipping a drink at an informal social gathering, a man walked over and engaged me in some light cocktail conversation. Obviously wanting to learn more about me—I had just become his minister—he asked where my father had gone to college, a frequent question of personal inquiry I would soon learn.

"He didn't," I responded. "My father didn't go to college."

"But he is an educated man, isn't he?" the man gasped.

I can do little to describe the incredulity that accompanied his words, short of mentioning his bulging eyes. He appeared as though he was either in the presence of a creature for whom he had great pity or from whom he was afraid he might contract some dreaded social disease.

Steve and I grew up in steel towns when steel was the biggest show in town—he in Youngstown, Ohio; I in Pittsburgh, Pennsylvania. Most of the people we knew worked in the mills, which included our fathers, grandfathers, other family members, and friends.

We were children of the hardworking, physically laboring, lower middle class. We didn't get invited to cocktail parties, but we did visit taverns where brass spittoons cluttered the floor; where jars of pickled eggs and canisters of Polish sausage sat on the smooth mahogany bars; and where burly men who worked the open hearth would toss down a boilermaker, or two, before starting their sweaty eight-hour shift.

Our culture was ethnic. We were surrounded by the descendants of immigrants—Poles, Czechs, Slavs, Serbs, Italians, and others who arrived here by way of Ellis Island. Russian was spoken in the home of Steve's maternal grandparents; German and Hungarian were spoken in the homes of my grandparents.

Steve and I didn't attend cotillion, and we knew nothing about the debutante ball. But we did attend a lot of wedding receptions in neighborhood fire halls where polkas were danced to accordion music and chunks of kielbasa were washed down with swigs of Iron City beer.

Daily life back then was characteristically physical, and disagreements too often were settled with fists instead of words. Corporal punishment was common in schools as well as homes. And there were experiences both of us were too embarrassed to admit after we left our hometowns and former lives behind.

Our fathers may not have had college degrees, but they sure wanted us to have them. And they, along with our mothers, worked extra-hard so we could go to school. Which we did—Ohio State for Steve, Penn State for me. Periodically, Steve and I would reminisce about those days and recall how damned lucky we felt to escape the mills and be the first in our families to earn a college degree.

So, Steve and I had different beginnings from most of the people we knew. And, yes, it mattered.

Both of us have been living in the South for a long time. More than forty years for me, a little less for Steve. We have adapted. This is home. But in the early years, certain adjustments had to be made, such as overcoming the language barrier.

One spring, Steve and I, along with two mutual friends, set out to do some fishing in the mountains near Boone, North Carolina. We were looking for a particular stream, but the directions we were given weren't working out. Some people will lie about such things, you know.

After a few wrong turns, we pulled up to a roadside store to ask for some help. Steve and I went inside, leaving the others in the car. We asked the guy behind the counter if he had heard of the stream. He said he had and told us where we missed our turn.

It was probably the first time either of us had heard a Southern Appalachian Mountain accent. The man's words took their time congealing. I envisioned putting a bucket under his chin to catch them as they oozed from his lips like maple syrup in the spring. Still and all, Steve and I swear the guy told us to go back down the road for a few miles and turn left at the *Snow Cone.* We thanked him and left.

After driving about ten miles, we wondered what he meant by "a few miles." Furthermore, there was nothing around us but woods. We hadn't seen a house for miles and wondered how a Snow Cone could possibly do any business way the hell out here. Finally, we decided to turn around and try the store again.

One of the men with us that day was a High Point lawyer, a North Carolina native who had hunted and fished all across the state.

"You all stay in the car and let me go in this time," Randy said. "Let me talk to him."

It wasn't two minutes before Randy came out of the store shaking his head and rolling his eyes. He opened the door and slid inside.

"You two Yankees," he said, looking first at Steve and then at me. "The guy said Sunoco. Turn left at the Sunoco…as in gas station."

The directions were good after we turned left at the Sunoco, which was three miles down the road. We found the stream with no trouble after that...and were thankful to have had an interpreter along.

Steve and I were a bit different. But that difference was part of what made us a good fit, part of what caused an office visit to evolve into an enduring friendship.

So here we are, standing in the parking lot outside a sandwich shop. We have just finished our meal and are walking to our cars. This is goodbye.

We have put this off until the last minute. Sunday will be my last day at the church—yet another goodbye. After the service and reception, Kathy and I will leave for our new home in Lynchburg, Virginia.

We stand for a moment by my car, the door half open. A lot has happened since the office visit that got this friendship going. Our children have grown up and are having children of their own. Relationships and friendships with others have been formed, and sometimes lost. Some who were close to us have died...or left us in one way or another, for one reason or another.

In a moment of reverie, I conjure an image of us as young men fishing together for the first time. Holding that image, I consider the two aging anglers we have become.

I think about how alike we are to those ephemeral mayflies we mimic in our attempts to trick the trout—the ones that emerge and fulfill their destinies in a burst of exuberance and purpose that passes all too quickly. I think, too, about how the most significant events in our lives ultimately lead us to goodbyes.

We shuffle our feet, give each other a stiff man-hug and say the words:

"See you, buddy."

"You, too. Stay in touch."

"I will. I'll call you in a week or so, after we get settled."

"Good. Let's plan a trip to the Holston sometime this summer."

"Let's do it. Bye now."

"So long."

I shut the door, start the engine, and pull away. As I turn onto the highway, I see Steve's car backing out from between two others. Before he passes out of view, I suddenly remember just how much I love to fish the Holston in the summer.

HOLY WATER

We have come a long way in this account, and I have not brought up one thing "religious." I have behaved myself. So indulge me...please...just this once; and I promise I won't do it again.

The specifically religious matter that keeps nagging me—and the reason I can't resist doing this—regards the mystical nature of water. Consider: unless we do it for a living, we don't *have* to fish, which is particularly true for those of us who practice catch and release. Surely there must be some primal instinct lodged deep within our souls that keeps bringing us back to the water's edge. After all, we originated in water. All life, all the way back to the earliest evolutionary microbes whose DNA resides inside our own, traces its origin to water.

Birth involves rising to the surface, our emergence from the pool of amniotic fluid in which we have lived like aquatic creatures inside our mother's core. And no matter what other interpretations attach to the ritual of baptism, it is clearly a symbolic reenactment of birth, where water once again serves as the medium through which a specific form of life—spiritual in this case—passes from one state to another.

Consider the fact that the Bible is awash in water stories. From the saga of Creation, to the Exodus, to Noah and Jonah, to Jesus and the Sea of Galilee, whenever cosmic events or personally transforming encounters occur, water is a character in the script—as it is in modern myths and metaphors, too.

We hardly need an anthropologist to explain the artist's portrayal of gathering clouds, or the musician's song about a bridge over troubled water. Legends, literary archetypes, and folklore—Moby Dick, Jaws, the Loch Ness Monster come to mind—could hardly persist without this primordial connection we humans have with water. It is our source. We tremble before its power and mystery. We regard it with awe and wonder. We endow it with holiness…holy water. We retreat to it, seeking from it solace, comfort, and renewal.

Early one spring, as Steve and I descended a curvy woodland path that brought us down from the jaunty little mountain stream we had been fishing, we ran into a motionless man staring at the ground. He turned out to be a professor of botany at a nearby university who was examining early blooming wildflowers. We chatted for a few minutes as he pointed out the objects of his concentration; then the three of us walked together the rest of the way down.

Periodically, the professor would stop dead in the path and point to shining blossoms decorating the drab forest floor. Steve and I would not have noticed them had it not been for the professor's trained and eager eyes. Enchantment framed his words as he described the unique characteristics of each plant and carefully pronounced both their common and Latin names.

The enthusiasm he showed toward his subjects quickly captured us, and by the time we reached the bottom of the mountain we had worn the poor professor out with questions: When do the plants bloom? Why do certain species grow in one place and not another? Where is the best place to find them? He proved to be as patient a teacher as he was a knowledgeable expert.

I don't remember how long it took for the three of us to get down the mountain, with all the stopping and looking and questioning along the way. Steve and I could have cared less about the time. And these many years later, we still talk about that evening when the forest became a grand cathedral—its intertwining branches soaring above us like sweeping arches, and the flowers, so delicate and bright against the brown earth, appearing as sacred objects commanding our reverence and respect.

The commingling components of the evening rendered it a revelatory occasion. Through a mundane occurrence—a walk in the woods—eternal truth momentarily pierced the veil of temporal experience, and human friendship, plants, fish, and water conspired to reveal the interconnectedness of all living things. Others may disagree, but that is what I would call a religious experience; and none of it would have occurred if Steve and I had not gone there in the first place...to the water.

A similar observation resulted from a decision Bill made to put a lake on some farm property he owns. He spent months researching the process and working up a design. Eventually, he contracted with professionals whose expertise and official authorization he needed, and the project moved forward in earnest.

A topographical survey determined the best location. Scrub brush and other vegetation were removed from the area. Then an access road was cut through to the site.

Next a bulldozer, accompanied by several other pieces of earth-moving equipment, rumbled in.

The machines manipulated the soil like potter's clay, creating the bowl that would capture the water from a small inflowing stream, several springs, and rain. Finally, the dozer fashioned the dam and plugged the open end.

When the heavy equipment rolled away, a great earthen cup waited to be filled. In its empty state, the lake-to-be was not a pretty sight. Barren, devoid of plant life, the place was muddy and forlorn. It looked like a scene from a natural disaster, or the aftermath of a military assault.

Bill turned the wheel that closed the valve at the bottom of the dam, and the cup began to fill. Each day he would measure its progress on a giant calibrated stick he had stabbed into the soil at the deepest end.

As the water rose, green shoots erupted on the lip of the cup and on the bare soil of the perimeter. Bill augmented nature's contribution by planting several hundred sawtooth oak seedlings on adjoining hills, and a variety of grasses on the dam and the gently sloping soil at the shallow end. In two months the lake was full.

Dave and I then joined Bill on trips to our favorite ponds, where—with permission—we caught bass and bream and transported them in large plastic coolers for relocation to their new home in Bill's lake. Several stockings of fathead minnows were added for forage, and later a truck outfitted with an aerated tank brought in a couple hundred rainbow trout.

The lake was born, and it was a beautiful sight to behold: lush, liquid, and teeming with life. The once-barren earth was covered in green. Insects danced their approval overhead, and ringlets of water marked the spots where the careless tarried a bit too long.

Turkey, deer, raccoon, ducks, bear, and other wildlife pressed their tracks into the soft soil along the banks. Sun, moon, and stars appeared in the lake's flat-mirrored face, and tall trees pushed and pulled their long, dark shadows across its surface, altering its complexion in the way theater lights enhance an actor's shifting mood.

Being a midwife to this birth was like being present at the moment of Creation. This singular event—the birth of a lake—seemed metaphoric of a general truth about the earth as a sacred and holy place.

We know from a mountain of research and anecdotal stories that close contact with people we do not know or understand often dispels the prejudices and misconceptions we have about them. Such awareness in turn makes it more difficult for us to objectify and mistreat them. Shouldn't we apply that same observation to our relationship with Mother Earth? Which leads me to wonder if sound and sane environmental laws would be so difficult to enact if more of us had intimate contact with her? Really intimate—the kind that results from close contact that is sensuous and direct.

If we did have that kind of contact, we might have second thoughts about draining marshlands to build another beachfront condominium, or removing acres of forest to shove in one more mountaintop resort, or finding convenient excuses to dump more poisons into our lakes, rivers, and streams.

These are not—to me, anyway—*just* environmental concerns, but they are spiritual issues rooted in the human soul. And I use the image deliberately. We are rooted in the earth, fed and nourished by it, in the way that any mother feeds a dependent child.

Ignore my spiritual biases if they offend, but at least consider the closeness of the bond, how, biologically speaking, we are one with the earth, sharing the same atoms, molecules, microbes, and historic evolution.

If there is a God (I am inclined to think there is reasonable evidence to think so), who created all that is, then it came as a package deal. We are not on the earth, but of the earth. And I can get downright anthropomorphic about that: seeing streams and rivers as the arteries and veins that course through the earth's outer skin, cleansing and nourishing it, keeping it alive; and we, the supposedly higher life-forms who originated in water—and still very much dependent upon it—as the progeny of this glorious and sacred living organism that has been entrusted to our care.

The waters of the earth—despite our considerable efforts to poison and disrupt them—are ripe with promise. Perhaps that belief, even if unconscious, is the deepest motivation that draws us to them. What other force could sustain our persistent, optimistic labors when we cast for sometimes hours, reaping neither fish nor strike?

Yet we persist. We persist because we believe that *something* is there. We remain hopeful. We are intrigued by the possibility that our efforts will ultimately prove worthwhile.

Would I be wrong to suggest that fishing—at least at times—may be an enacted metaphor dramatizing the human desire to believe? One that reflects our unquenchable desire to connect with a timeless creative source that gives meaning and purpose to our lives? Even the line that attaches us to the mysteries of the water implies a connection between our world of temporal senses and the ineffable reality that exists beyond the limitations of space and time.

The smallest mountain stream—such as the one on which Steve and I met the botanist—eventually makes its way to the sea. You could say from a limited perspective that what is seen of that stream within one small slice of time is gone forever. And you would be right. But from a more expansive perspective, you would also be right in claiming that it never dies.

Throughout its long journey, the stream we saw changes form: from stream to river to bay to ocean to vapor to rain…and back again, endless and eternal. Its outward visible appearance transforms. Its molecules segue from one physical arrangement to another. Even when it mingles with the great oceans, its essence remains. None of it is lost.

Well, there I go drawing parallels again. But I did promise that if you let me get by with preaching just this once, I wouldn't do it again. So I won't press my luck or try your patience. Besides, the water does a better job of proclaiming the majesty of God than I do, anyway.

Amen.

Smith River Memories

Steve and I arranged to meet at the convenience store near the Bassett exit off Route 220. He would be driving north, from High Point; I would be coming south, from Lynchburg. We had not seen much of each other since I retired, and were looking forward to getting together for some fishing on the Smith River.

We began fishing the Smith more than thirty years ago. It was the closest major trout stream to our High Point homes, and in the early days of our friendship we fished it often. Back then, the Smith was a first-rate river. *Trout* magazine, in its 1989 "Special Anniversary Series," listed it as one of America's one hundred best trout streams.

Today, the Smith is not even a particularly good trout stream. I understand that fish biologists are looking into it, but nobody official seems to know what happened, or why. When the fishing started falling off, Steve and I cut back on the number of trips we made. In recent years, we hardly fished the Smith at all.

I arrived at the meeting spot first, parked in a shady patch at the far end of the parking lot, and waited for Steve to arrive. In a few minutes he pulled alongside. We greeted, transferred his gear to my truck, and headed down the two-lane road that follows the river into the town of Bassett.

I had always thought Bassett would make a good setting for a Steinbeck novel, but now it looked even more like a retrospect of the Great Depression. The effects of the national economic collapse and the deterioration of the furniture industry—Bassett's economic base—were obvious.

The one-story frame houses lining the road into town were more in need of paint than ever. The restaurant where Steve and I had stopped for morning coffee and eaten so many meals after a long day on the water was dark. Its parking lot was empty.

A furniture factory we passed looked like an abandoned tenement. One of its main buildings—a hulking, multistoried structure that used to bustle with activity—was silent. Not a single worker was about. The town had changed since our last visit, and not for the better.

The three-mile special regulation section was where we had done most of our fishing, and we saw no need to change. To get there, we drove along a decaying asphalt road that services a string of sad houses surrounded by cluttered yards and aging cars. Just before the road dead-ended, we turned onto a bumpy dirt path and parked by the railroad tracks that parallel the river.

We wiggled into our waders, strung up the rods, and started to walk upstream—by way of the tracks. We were looking for the path that used to wind through the thick brush and down to the river's edge. We missed it on the first pass and thought it must have filled in from lack of use. But after backtracking and poking among the high weeds, we found it—somewhat overgrown, but passable.

"It's still a beautiful river," Steve said, as we stepped off the bank.

"Yes, it is," I agreed, "as beautiful as ever."

Despite its brief passage through Bassett, the Smith cuts a winding swath through mostly rural landscape. Its banks are lined with tall hardwoods and dense shrubs, and few buildings are visible from the water. There are a thousand places along the Smith that could provide photographs for an office calendar depicting monthly scenes of America's natural beauty.

Steve and I have undergone noticeable physical changes over the past thirty years—a bit heavier, less hair, more aches and pains, not as agile, etc., etc.—but the Smith seemed to have hardly changed at all. As we made our way upstream we saw rocks, runs, riffles, and pools that we had seen a hundred times before.

Certain recognizable trees stood like sentries along the riverbanks. The meandering curves of the river unfolded in predictable succession, one after another, like well-known verses in a childhood poem. Pocket water and deep pools showed up at their appointed places, and the slant of the surrounding hills was as familiar as the face of an old friend.

Since our first trip to the Smith, Steve and I have raised children, become grandfathers, practiced our professions, built reputations, dealt with a potful of life's ups and downs, and arrived at a place on the vitality continuum where most of our active years are visible in the rearview mirror. Yet, whatever route our lives were traveling at the time, the Smith was somewhere in the scenery. It was the place we went to relax, to escape from whatever pressures were bearing down on us. It was the place we went to celebrate, to think, to laugh, and, sometimes, to heal.

In the summer of 1995, when I needed to take a six-week leave of absence because of a serious bout of clinical depression, Steve and another friend dogged me to go with them for an evening on the Smith. At that point in my recovery, I didn't have the energy or motivation to go anywhere. But they persisted, and I agreed.

As Steve and I fished our way upriver, I recalled that day. I remembered the pall of lethargy that hung on me like a lead cape. I remembered the heavy effort necessary to put one foot in front of the other. I remembered how I stopped fishing at one point and sat on a large, flat-topped boulder in the middle of the river; how I lingered there listening to the sounds of the breeze and the birds and the river running by.

I remembered how calming and peaceful those moments were…and how hopeful. And I remembered how prominently they featured in the reawakening of my mood and my spirit.

As we passed by it, I recognized that rock, protruding like an ancient monument from the water that swirled around it. I was grateful for what it had done for me, and even more grateful that—on this occasion—I had no need to sit and rest upon it.

Later, we passed the place where we had once made a hasty and unplanned exit from the river, clambering up the bank with rising water nipping at our butts. Because the Smith is a tailrace river, its rate of flow is regulated by a hydroelectric dam. The authorities in charge post a schedule as to when they are going to release enough water to drive the heavy turbines. This is an essential piece of information to have when fishing the Smith. When the floodgates open and they are "generating," the water level rises several feet—quickly. And when it does, you don't want to be caught waist-deep in the middle of the river.

One of us had checked the schedule, but the recorded announcement does add a disclaimer that says it is "subject to change without notice." Whether the schedule changed without notice or we didn't listen carefully made no practical difference. The water started coming at us like high tide, and we knew we had about sixty seconds to either find a surfboard or get out.

Unfortunately, we were on the wrong side of the river—meaning the river was between us and our transportation home. We made a futile attempt at crossing, but the current drove us back, forcing us to claw our way up the bank like two bloated crabs as the river swelled behind us like a spring flood.

The way back to the truck was going to require a long walk downstream to the bridge, then another just as long upstream to the parking spot: several miles of walking…in waders and bulky vests.

As we neared the bridge, a cluster of small houses picketed by an array of unwelcoming signs blocked our path. The *No Trespassing* ones didn't bother us much; we figured the judge would appreciate our predicament. But the *Beware of Dog* ones were another matter, especially since two scruffy crossbred specimens were lounging in a dense shadow next to one of the houses, yawning and swatting flies with their frizzled tails.

Steve and I put on our best alpha male faces and strode confidently forward, through the yards and past the dogs. It wasn't like we had a choice. Fortunately, it turned out to be a good day for trespassing. The canines left us alone, and their owners never appeared. I am sure we exhaled by the time we reached the bridge.

With these and other memories as companions, Steve and I leisurely fished our way farther up the river. We caught trout: not a lot, and nothing large. But some of those fish rose to our flies in the exact places where others had in years past.

There is a particular place on the river where—for some strange hydraulic reason—it curves in a way that forces the main current to the center while forming a wide band of slower water that eases smoothly past the outside bend. The trees on that side lean out over the river, dangling their branches over the surface like trellis vines. Attempting to cast underneath them is likely to result in a tangled mess. Most anglers skip the hazard and fish the unobstructed center channel instead.

But if you are left-handed, as I am, you have a better angle to sneak an upstream cast under those fly-snagging limbs. As I edged closer to the spot, I recalled some of the fish I had caught there, and couldn't pass it up.

A #20 Parachute Adams had worked before—why not now? I knotted it to the tippet and flipped it under the fluttering leaves. The Adams settled and began a slow, semicircular ride around the bend. As it curled back in my direction, the surface erupted, and a good trout sucked it under.

The trout was no trophy, but handsome. Bright red spots glimmered like points of light on brown flanks that melted into golden sunlight as they wrapped around the fish's underside. I looked just long enough to appreciate the art, then tweaked the fly and watched the palette of colors swim away—just as I had done so many times before.

Around one o'clock, Steve's back was acting up. He had been a good athlete in his youth—even contemplated a career in professional baseball before an arm injury altered his plans and he settled into medicine—but the wear and tear of the years and the games have taken their toll. Now he can fish for only about three hours before discomfort outweighs the fun.

When he hit the three-hour mark, he reeled in and headed for the truck. I kept fishing, but knowing Steve was waiting needled my conscience; after another half-hour of guilty pleasure I, too, called it a day.

We drove back to the restaurant, hoping that the morning's closure indicated only reduced hours and it might be open for lunch. No such luck.

This second attempt prompted Steve to ask if I remembered the young woman who worked there when we started coming to the Smith. She would have been eighteen, nineteen at the time, a student at Virginia Tech. Her family owned the place, and she came home weekends to wait on customers. Outgoing and flush with youth's envious possibilities, she would stand by our table and tell us of her plans and dreams.

The business had changed hands several times since then, and we lost contact with her years ago. But we were wondering if she had made good on her ambitions…and hoped she had. "You know," I pointed out, "she'd be in her forties now."

We were disappointed that the restaurant wasn't open. We would have enjoyed eating there again, for old times' sake. But the truth is: While it was the same building, the restaurant we knew didn't exist anymore.

That was the one that made the best baked beans we had ever eaten. Juicy and stewed in a sauce rich with onions and spices, they were served steaming—in a pint-size Styrofoam cup. We have never had their equal. Not even close.

It was also the place where we could order "thumb ice cream" for dessert. The restaurant didn't call it that, of course; Steve and I did because of the way it was served.

The lady who scooped our designated flavors from the deep circular containers had her own unique method of transferring each dollop from scoop to cone. She used her thumb. Thus, each creamy ball bore her distinguishing mark, like a signed portrait.

Disappointed that we weren't going to be able to reminisce about beans and ice cream, we decided to try the Hardees's in the next town over. We pulled onto the river road and left Bassett behind.

As we munched on burgers and fries, we caught up on what each of us had been doing and what we knew about mutual friends and acquaintances. Our trip to the Smith had been a touchstone connecting the present to the past.

Our day on the river was like reconnecting with a steadfast friend who had been with us through some of the most important passages of our lives. And for more reasons than fishing, the Smith had earned a place of permanence among the memories we will carry with us into whatever future lies before us on our journey to the final cast.

After we ate, I drove Steve back to his car. He placed his gear in the trunk and stuck out his hand: "It's been a good day."

"Sure has," I replied. "We need to do this again."

Steve nodded in agreement. In the silence that passed between us I sensed mutual awareness of the finite amount of time allotted for such things.

Then we left for home. Steve drove south, and I turned north.

Dogs

If it turns out there really is a heaven—in whatever counterintuitive form it might take—*surely,* there will be a place for dogs.

One reason I value the friendship of my fishing buddies is that their dogs have told me what good men they are. You can learn a lot about a man from the way he interacts with his dog. Michael Vick can play football again for all I care: he's paid his debt to society. But I'll be damned if I'd ever fish with him.

Most of our guys have been dog men for years. Jimmy had a Brittany spaniel named Copper, whom he took to work when he owned his fly shop in Charlottesville. She was such a good-natured and friendly bitch that Jim decided to bring her along on one of our fishing trips. None of the rest of us knew about the invitation until she jumped out of the Jeep.

This was back in our camping days, when we were cooking over a wood fire and sleeping in tents. Copper was a young pup then, frisky and curious—which was all right, even entertaining, until it was time for bed.

Jim was sharing a tent with Dave, and when it came time to retire, Copper curled up at the foot of Jim's sleeping bag. But the prolific smells and noises of the nighttime forest pushed poor Copper's self-restraint beyond its limits.

Jim did his best to settle her down: "Copper, hush. Lie down, Copper; be a good dog."

Dave, who had been awakened several times by a variety of Copper's plaintive outbursts, drew on his knowledge of dog obedience training: "Copper, shut the — up." The rest of us, who were trying to sleep in nearby tents, can attest to the enthusiasm with which the exchanges between dog and men took place, before they were brought to an abrupt end.

After a few hours of whimpering, woofing, and pawing at the zippered tent flap, Dave could stand no more. He unzipped the opening and pushed her out. Thrilled to be liberated, Copper shot off into the night and was neither seen nor heard until the next morning.

She ambled into camp while we were cooking breakfast, wearing that wide-eyed, open-mouthed expression dogs have when they are smiling. Unlike the previous evening, she was calm. Her breathing was unhurried, and her tail swished in slow undulating rhythm, like a palm branch swaying in a soft coastal breeze. You can tell a lot about a dog from the wagging of its tail.

Now I know there are experts who will tell you that dogs don't have the range of emotional expression I am ascribing to Copper; that what is actually going on is we humans are merely projecting our own feelings onto the animal and reading back what we want to see. Well, I have observed enough dog tails and witnessed sufficient doggy smiles to assure you Copper was a very contented dog.

Later in the morning, Dave ran into some guys who were camped upriver from us. One asked if he had seen a brown and white Brittany. He said the damn dog had come into their camp during the night, got into their stuff, rattled through their pots and pans, ate some of their food, and kept them awake half the night. Dave thanked him for the warning and said he would be on the lookout.

Copper was no better at being a fishing companion than she was a camp guest. Jimmy brought her along when he, Dave, and I drove over the mountain to fish one of our favorite sections of Back Creek in southwestern Virginia, just south of the West Virginia line.

When Jim opened the Jeep door, Copper launched. This was one fast dog. Before we could fish any pool, Copper had already been there. She would plunge into the water, swim a few splashy laps, then circle back toward us, running so fast her ears were horizontal to the ground.

Copper was having a marvelous time. You could tell from her bright, toothy smile. Dave, on the other hand, was not smiling. You can tell a lot about Dave from how he's not smiling.

When Copper cavorted through a particularly promising run that Dave was about to fish, another session of obedience training commenced. This time the verbal commands were accompanied by a few sticks lobbed in Copper's direction.

It mattered not. Copper was having far too good a time to be discouraged by curses and a few flimsy sticks flung her way—all of which fell way wide of their mark in any case. The dog was just too maneuverable. In fact, she must have considered the whole thing a game: with each hurled stick and insult, Copper's smile grew wider.

With Copper racing about while we humans tried to slip in a quick cast before she was back in the water, it was inevitable that the trajectory of fly and dog would intersect. As I fired a cast into a small circle of pocket water,

Copper jumped in just as the fly hit the water, hooking her solidly in a wad of fur along her flank.

The hook didn't penetrate Copper's flesh, which was fortunate—sort of. I mean fortunate that Copper wasn't wounded; but not so fortunate in that she didn't realize she was now attached to my fly line.

The reel screeched as Copper tore off to her next destination, streaming line behind her as she went. I raced after her, desperately trying to keep up, like those salmon fishermen in Alaska who sprint along the riverbanks, trying to keep pace with some fifty-pound fish they have on the line. Only I was in pursuit of a dog. I am glad no one was around except Dave and Jim; the whole scene must have looked ridiculous.

The three of us eventually corralled Copper long enough to extract the fly, but by that time we were panting like racehorses, and our tongues hung out farther than the dog's. We were finished, spent. Besides, there wasn't a fish within a mile that hadn't gone into hiding.

We reeled in and walked back to the truck. With no one to throw sticks or play chase, Copper followed along and willingly jumped into the back seat—hoping no doubt that we were transporting her to the next great adventure.

We kept Jim out of the deliberations—due to his obvious conflict of interest—but the rest of us discussed the situation and then voted. Following a presentation of the evidence, a unanimous decision was rendered: Copper was convicted...blackballed...banished...never to be allowed on one of our fishing trips again.

We informed Jim of the sentence, which he took a little more personally than expected. Copper, on the other hand, didn't seem to care one way or the other. She just sat next to Jim, smiling as he stroked her head. Dave, I noticed, was smiling, too.

Bill is more of a hunter than a fisherman. He particularly enjoys duck hunting, and he once had a golden retriever named Bullet, who was his favorite hunting companion. All Bill had to say was "Bullet, come," and Bullet would bound into the front seat of Bill's truck.

Bill and Bullet were such staunch buddies that Bullet would often accompany Bill even when they weren't hunting. It wasn't uncommon to see Bill's truck coming down the road with Bullet on the seat beside him, like two commuters on their way to the office.

Bill loved that dog, and still talks about him the way some of us brag about our grandchildren. Bullet died about ten years ago, after a dedicated career of retrieving Bill's downed ducks. But there was one episode in his storied life that stands out above all the others.

Bill took a friend along when he and Bullet went duck hunting on the James River near Snowden, Virginia. The man didn't realize that Bullet was out of the boat when he took a shot at a wounded bird that was flopping on the surface. Bullet had already reached the bird, and when the man fired, he hit Bullet.

Bill pulled his bleeding dog into the boat and took off for the vet. When I asked Bill and his wife to describe what they remembered about the incident, Kitty told me how Bill had called her from the vet's office, in tears, to let her know that Bullet had been shot. The only reason that detail is important is that Bill is a get-it-done, straight-ahead kind of guy—definitely not the crying type. Kitty also remembered how Bill looked when he came home, the front of his shirt covered in blood. Bill had cradled

Bullet in his arms as he carried him back to the truck, which was no small effort, considering Bullet weighed 112 pounds, and it was uphill most of the way.

The vet performed emergency surgery, and Bullet recovered from his wounds—except for one eye, which was damaged beyond repair. It took Bullet about six months of bumping into objects before he got used to seeing with just one eye. But eventually he was back at Bill's side, riding next to him in the truck, and retrieving ducks back to the boat.

Bill told me he has owned dogs that had better noses, even dogs that were better retrievers than Bullet; but he was emphatic when he told me that he's never owned a better dog. You can tell a lot about a man—and his dog—by the loyalty they show each other.

Bill was understanding about the incident and forgave the man who shot Bullet. "It was an accident," he said, "and the guy was devastated." Now that's character, the kind of character that even dogs recognize.

Steve once owned two high-spirited yellow Labs. When I stopped by the house, they would gambol to the door, greeting me with exuberant wiggling and bowing, much tail wagging, and a cascade of slobbery kisses I would have gladly done without. They were a jocular pair, with an irrepressible penchant for mischief.

One weekend, Steve and his family had out-of-town plans and arranged for a neighbor to come by and look after the dogs, which were to be confined in a spacious garage where they would have food, water, and beds. When Steve and his family returned on Sunday evening, they were greeted at the front door by their two frolicking pets.

Steve was initially perturbed that the dog-sitter had carelessly let his charges into the house, when the explicit instructions had been that they be confined to the garage. When Steve entered the den, he realized that the sitter had done nothing wrong.

The den shared a wall with the garage. The two miscreant dogs, eager to get back into the house from which they had been banned, spent their weekend of confinement pawing at the sheetrock until they made a hole large enough to put their powerful jaws to work. By the time Steve and his family returned, the job was complete: they had widened the hole sufficiently to perform the canine version of *The Great Escape*. They wiggled through the opening, and the house was theirs.

One of the dogs, Cirion, also had a taste for carpet. Only Steve with his extensive medical training can tell this story with sufficient clinical detail, but I'll do my best.

For whatever exotic taste sensation motivated her, Cirion ate a substantial portion of braided rug. In this case, her usual partner in crime, Boswell, did not join in the repast. While it is hard to imagine, even for a dog, Cirion painstakingly swallowed yard-long strands of carpet, much like you or I might do when sucking down a length of pasta.

The gastrointestinal anatomy of a dog allows for a rather straight passage: what comes in one end goes out the other. And since carpet fibers don't digest well—actually not at all—they came out Cirion's back end the same way they came in the front—intact, one long strand at a time.

Steve said that for the better part of a week, Cirion was in acute anal distress. She would defecate—a more frequent activity due to the amount of carpet consumed—and the only thing she could show for the effort would be a partially extracted strand of fiber that would dangle from her sphincter. Fortunately, the trailing textile was of sufficient length that Steve—if he moved quickly enough—could step on it. The remainder would then extrude through Cirion's rectum as she trotted off. (I hope this is not too much detail.)

After a week or so of Steve's stepping on protruding fibers, his ministrations proved successful, and Cirion was finally void of carpet. A dog may be man's best friend, but this story has convinced me that the relationship works both ways.

I have a long-standing relationship with my own dog, McKinley, our convivial English cocker spaniel. He's over fourteen, and people still mistake him for a puppy. With his soulful brown eyes and stately head, he's a handsome boy. He has good bloodlines, too, and probably could have been one of those prissy show dogs if he had learned to dress better. This dog cares nothing about appearance, and I am beginning to suspect that he might be a redneck, despite his aristocratic pedigree.

Clean him up, and he'll go right out in the yard and roll in the dirt—all the while with one of those big doggy smiles on his face. And the way he sprawls on the floor makes him look like he should have a Budweiser in his paw. He's just a slob.

My wife and I once took him to a park to swim, one of his favorite things to do. After he had swum to his satisfaction, he located a copious mound of horse droppings along the trail and rolled in them until he was covered with scent. Realizing what he had done, I made McKinley go for another swim. But horse poop, when it's wet and gooey, is tenacious stuff. It seeped into McKinley's fur and clung like paste. We tried wiping him down, which only massaged the mixture deeper into his coat.

We rode home with the windows open, for all the good it did. There is no recipe for odor quite like that of wet spaniel basted in horseshit and warmed inside an un-air-conditioned car. It was a long hour's drive home for Kathy and me. McKinley didn't seem to mind at all.

I have to confess, there are times—such as when my wife asks me why I am not more concerned about my appearance—that I really empathize with my dog. You could even say we are a lot alike in the way neither of us has much of an eye for fashion.

McKinley and I took a walk the other day, and we ran into a most attractive woman and her dog. I couldn't help but notice how impeccably dressed the woman was: pressed preppie blouse and shorts, new sandals, mani-cured nails, and a trim, fashionable haircut. McKinley, I am sure, noticed the same thing about her dog, which looked like it had just come from the spa. Its soft fur was so clean it fluttered as it walked.

McKinley was already way past his grooming date, which only added to his beggarly appearance when he emerged from under the bushes he had been sniffing. Grass and pieces of leaves clung to his coat. His paws were muddy, and a smudge of dirt covered half his nose. A string of drool dangling from his lower lip completed his ensemble.

I didn't look so good myself. It was a hot day, I had just mowed the lawn, and it didn't make sense to show-er until I had walked the dog—or, obviously, to change clothes, either. I was still wearing a pair of soiled khaki pants, a sweat-stained T-shirt, and a disgusting pair of beat-up yard shoes that looked like they had been retrieved from the dump.

In our mutually wretched condition, McKinley and I stood facing this elegant woman and her beautiful dog. As we chatted, I couldn't help but wonder if she had ever heard that old saying, the one about how you can tell a lot about a man from the appearance of his dog.

HOSTILE TERRITORY

The first thing I noticed was the stick sailing in my direction, which was followed by several more. Wanting to give the guy the benefit of the doubt, I thought he might not understand that throwing large chunks of dead branches in the water scares the fish. Then I decided he must be a jerk.

Before I had a chance to sort out which of these two conclusions I wanted to go with, he clarified the matter. His stick-lobbing having drawn no response from me, he let fly with a tirade of verbal abuse. The guy was angry, red-faced-mean angry.

It took me a minute to figure out what was going on; then I remembered I was on the Jackson River, near Covington, Virginia. At the time, a major dispute was making its way through the courts regarding how much control certain landowners had over the water that flowed through their property.

Referring to antique deeds issued by Kings George II and George III—called crown grants—the landowners claimed that possessing such a deed granted the holder exclusive ownership of the river bottom and the fish above it. In practical terms, that meant no one could wade the river where it passed through their land. Because the Jackson had been officially designated a navigable stream, boaters could not be prevented from floating through, but they had better not anchor, fish, swim, or leave their boats for any reason.

The case reached the courts when a well-known fishing guide from the area challenged the claim, allowing his clients to continue fishing as they passed through "crown grant" water. He was arrested and charged with trespassing.

The situation created a strange conundrum for fishermen: the commonwealth of Virginia had built kiosks at entry points to the river, and regularly stocked it with trout. Many wondered how a private landowner could claim exclusive rights to fish that had been stocked by the state. Others found it a curiosity that grants dating back to English kings would still be valid, especially in a state that featured so prominently in the Revolutionary War.

The issue generated purple editorial prose in local papers and heated, in-your-face personal exchanges. I even heard anecdotal reports of weapons being brandished. A lot of stories and rumors were going around at the time. In any case, there was no doubt that the atmosphere was charged with incendiary discontent.

The case wound its way through the lower courts until a series of appeals propelled it all the way to the Virginia Supreme Court. The justices, in what many believe was a politically influenced decision, rendered a controversial four-to-three verdict supporting the validity of crown grants. Other landowners—those not holding a crown grant—could not exercise the same level of control over the river. Go figure.

My encounter with the stick hurler took place well before the final decision, when the issue was still being debated in the public press and litigated in the courts. As far as I was concerned, it was still legal to fish until a final ruling came down. The man yelling at me from across the river had a different interpretation. He was intent on getting me off "his" river and intimidating me with his bullying, should I ever consider passing that way again.

The guy was losing it, and I sometimes wonder what might have happened had the river not been between us. But fishing is supposed to be fun, so I kept my mouth shut, reeled in, and walked away. Heck, I thought, he has already screwed up the fishing; no sense letting him up-end my tranquility as well.

I have never come close to getting into a fight on a trout stream, but it would be hard to fish for as many decades as I have without running into provocations that could have turned ugly under different circumstances. So far, thankfully, the good fairy of restraint has helped me keep my mouth shut and kept me out of trouble.

Steve and I make frequent trips to eastern Tennessee, particularly to fish the South Holston River. We love that river and its surrounding countryside, but are frequently baffled by the amount of trash deposited along the river's banks. On our way from truck to river, we have walked past stacks of garbage bags, broken toilets, castoff sofas, battered refrigerators, and all sorts of rejected household goods. "Why do people do that?" is a constant refrain. "Wouldn't it be just as easy to carry that crap to the land-fill as to the river?" It really gets under our skin.

I was getting out of the water one evening, ready to call it a day, when a much-abused pickup with dented fenders and scarred paint pulled onto the shoulder of the road. It could not have been more than twenty feet from where I crested the bank.

The driver got out and gave me a quick glance before stepping to the edge of the road, where he unzipped and proceeded to pee like a fire hydrant. His initial task complete, he strutted around to the bed of the truck, where he locked his eyes on mine before reaching in and pulling out a large, black trash bag.

The top was choked closed with a wire twist, and the sides bulged in slanting angles where the generous load inside strained against the plastic film. The man cocked his arm back, twisted his body around to the right, and with a mighty heave sent the bag flying out over the riverbank. I watched as it rose in a semicircular trajectory before curving downward, crashing to the ground with a mingled sound of crunching boxes and rattling cans.

I turned toward the man, who was still staring at me...with challenge in his eyes. Men know that look— the focused gaze that sends their wordless message: I dare you to say something. And I did want to say something. I very much wanted to say something. But I didn't.

I turned away and started breaking down my rod. I heard a door slam and knew the litterer had gotten into his truck. In a spray of yellow dust that plumed behind, it bumped back onto the asphalt and sped away.

If that brief encounter had been a comic strip, there would have been a balloon above my head containing the words I thought of saying, but didn't. "Asshole" would have been among them. Sometimes silence is the wiser choice.

So far, I have avoided being assaulted on a trout stream. I have also avoided being shot, which brings me to another situation that could have turned out differently.

It was a crisp, fall weekend in early December—deer season—when Steve and I decided to fish Whitetop Laurel Creek in Washington County, Virginia, one more time before cold weather set in. We drove up Friday night in time to set up our tent in a campground already filled with hunters. Most had been there since early in the week. Some had already gotten their deer, as evidenced by the ones that were gutted and hanging to drain in nearby trees.

The next morning, on our way into town for breakfast, we passed several trucks with fresh-killed deer lying in the back or draped over hoods. We saw hunters in town and along the roads, and we knew that most were still in the woods, where they had been since dawn.

Steve and I drove to the river, put our rods together, and agreed to meet back at the truck by noon. He was going to walk downstream several hundred yards and fish his way back; I said I would fish upriver and take the road back.

The river was low and clear, not unusual for the fall, but we'd had an exceptionally dry summer, which made it particularly so. The fish get hyper-nervous under such conditions, and it doesn't take much to send them scurrying under the nearest rock.

I knew if I was going to deceive any fish at all, stealth and slow methodical wading would be essential. All morning, as I worked my way upstream, I stayed close to the edges, using the trees and shadows for concealment. I had dressed for the conditions—fall colors and earth tones to blend with tree trunks, fallen leaves, and the exposed forest floor.

I hunched as I walked, bending at the waist so the fish would not be alarmed by a silhouette moving across the backlit sky. I lifted each leg carefully so I wouldn't send ripples across the water. I stalked like an animal, confident in my predatory skills.

This reverie of conceit was interrupted by the crack of five loud rifle shots. They came in rapid succession, hardly a second between each one. Whoever was firing was not shooting at me—I was sure of that; but the shots did come from a place nearby, and their number scared me. I don't hunt, but Bill does. And he's good at it. He would be embarrassed if he missed on the first shot, and I doubt that he would even take a second. Five rounds squeezed off so rapidly indicated either a bad shot or a desperate hunter—or worse, both.

It was almost noon when I heard the shots, so I was glad to have a reason to get off the water and take the road back to the truck. Steve was already there when I arrived.

We leaned our rods against a tree, and sat on the tailgate while we ate our lunch. As we were cleaning up and putting the cooler away, a pickup pulled in beside us.

It slid to a stop, and three twenty-something men jumped out. Beers in hand, they asked us how the fishing had been. They were a jovial and friendly group, like so many country boys I've known. They downed the last of the beer, and tossed the empties into the bed of the truck on top of the layer of cans that preceded them.

One of the young men folded the front seat forward and pulled out their rifles, then passed a box of cartridges around. Each of the young men took a handful, filled their magazines, and stuffed the rest into the pockets of their coats. They wished us good luck with our fishing and left, joking and jostling as they disappeared into the woods.

Steve and I looked at the boys, and then at our rods, still resting against a tree. I wasn't sure what he was thinking, but I was recalling an article I had read about the human capacity to distort perception—that is, how we see what we want to see when we are desperate to see it. Like hunters who mistake cows and dogs—and other hunters—for deer.

I was also thinking about how animal-like I had tried to look while stalking trout earlier that morning—bent over, dressed in brown, moving cautiously…wearing that old, felt wide-brim hat that might be mistaken for antlers by someone desperate enough to think so. These thoughts passed through my mind in a millisecond. They included sound effects: the crack of five shots and the thud of beer cans hitting the bed of a truck.

Before I had a chance to say anything, I heard Steve's voice: "Want to call it a day?"

"Why not," I said. "We have a long drive home."

That is one of the stories we recall when our group gets together, but when the beers are passed around and we start telling stories about unpleasant experiences on the water, there is no argument that Steve's wins the blue ribbon prize. It began when he heard an authoritative voice behind his back: "Put your hands in the air and don't turn around."

Steve raised his hands, but—he must have been curious or terrified—he turned around anyway. There stood the sheriff, along with two deputies—whose guns were drawn and pointed at Steve.

"Don't move," the sheriff commanded. "Stay right where you are."

Steve had made a solo trip to the Roanoke River in eastern North Carolina to fish the annual shad run. Because that involved more than a day trip from High Point, he had booked a room at a motel near the river, and planned to spend two days pursuing the shad. The fact that he had come by himself proved to be a serious complication in his unexpected encounter with the law.

"What are you doing here?" asked the sheriff.

"I'm fishing," Steve replied, a touch of irony in his voice. Attired in fishing gear with a rod in his hand seemed to make the answer pretty obvious, he thought.

"Do you have any identification?" was the sheriff's next question.

Steve noted from the sheriff's no-nonsense attitude that something heavy must be going down, but figured that once the lawman learned who he was the matter would be quickly resolved and apologies extended.

Lowering his hands carefully, so as not to excite the deputies, he reached inside his pocket and retrieved his wallet. He stated his full name and address as he handed over his license, adding, "I am a physician; I practice in High Point."

The sheriff studied the license, and looked back and forth several times between Steve and the picture on the laminated card. There was no question Steve was who he said he was, but that didn't seem to matter.

"When did you leave High Point, and how long have you been in this area?"

The sheriff was becoming more interrogative, and Steve's initial shock and irritation at being confronted like a criminal were now evolving into fear and incredulity.

"Do you mind telling me what's going on here?" he asked.

"A child was molested not far from here," the sheriff answered. "And you match the description of the assailant. Would you please answer the question?"

"I am a doctor, for God's sake," Steve said. "You can call my office and check."

No doubt having been trained that child predators come from all stations of life and have an artful ability to rationalize and dissemble, the sheriff was not swayed by Steve's credentials. He pressed on.

"When did you leave High Point, and can you account for your whereabouts since?"

Steve was trying to recall his itinerary, but you know what it's like when someone puts you on the spot and asks you to recall unimportant details you don't ordinarily give much thought to—especially when two sour-faced deputies are standing next to you with guns in their hands.

Steve stammered as he tried to collect his thoughts. "Let's see. I left High Point around four o'clock yesterday afternoon, stopped to get a sandwich along the way, checked into the motel, got up this morning, came over to the river, where I've been all day."

"Can anyone verify how long you have been here fishing?"

"I came by myself," Steve explained. "I saw a few guys on the water, said hello, but I didn't know any of them." The answer was clearly insufficient.

"Sir, we are going to have to take you with us for some further questioning."

Steve was beginning to panic. Then he thought to ask, "When did the molestation take place?"

"Between ten and ten thirty this morning," said the sheriff.

"I was still at the motel then!" Steve shot back, relieved to finally have a foothold. "I got up, ate some breakfast, got my fishing gear together, and didn't leave the motel until almost eleven."

"Can you verify that you were at the motel?"

Steve remembered that he had checked in with a credit card. "Here," he said, eagerly handing over the receipt.

"Can anyone substantiate that? Did you talk to anyone?"

Steve remembered that he had spoken with the manager at the desk. But the sheriff was not about to take his word for it.

"OK, let's drive over there and check that out."

The officers accompanied Steve to the motel, where the manager confirmed his alibi. He had not only seen Steve, but remembered when he left for the river. The time frame, along with the distance between the motel and the place of the crime, made it impossible for Steve to be the man the sheriff was looking for. That having been established, Steve was released. The sheriff apologized for the inconvenience, wished him good fishing for the remainder of the trip, and turned toward the door, his deputies trailing along.

Steve watched them pull away, and thought about driving back to the river to resume the shad fishing he had been looking forward to for months. He still had the rest of the day and most of the next. But being nearly arrested on false charges of child abuse tends to suck the enjoyment out of a trip. Instead, he canceled the room reservation, paid the bill, packed up his gear, and got on the road back to High Point.

I expect that every member of our group, to the man, will tell you that he has met some of the finest people he knows through fishing, and had some of the best times of his life while doing it. But, there are those rare occasions when …. Well, life's too short to dwell on that.

ALL ABOUT DAVE

On his sixtieth birthday, I gave Dave a post.

Dave's wife, Beth, who organized the party honoring six decades of Dave's gregarious life, had given explicit instruction that there were to be no gifts. Cards and gag gifts were allowed.

The post was white, made of PVC, and measured six feet long. With a ball cap on top and a fish-print tie secured with a full Windsor at the center, it looked quite respectable: the perfect gift for Dave, I thought. And from the comments I received, others thought so, too.

Dave was born and raised in wild and wonderful West Virginia. Actually, he was born just over the line in Clifton Forge, Virginia. But that was a minor geographical technicality due to the level of health care in West Virginia in the 1940s. I won't elaborate, beyond mentioning that this is the state that once rejoiced exceedingly when it moved from fiftieth to forty-ninth on a national scale of socioeconomic standings. I believe Mississippi took bottom honor that year.

When the time came for Dave to be delivered, his father loaded the Missis in the car and made the thirty-mile drive from Lewisburg to Clifton Forge, where the closest hospital with adequate birthing facilities was to be found. In a few days, the three of them made the return trip. So, while Dave's birth certificate may say "Virginia," trust me, he is West Virginia, through and through.

Regional accents and colloquialisms are dead give-aways when it comes to pinning down someone's place of origin. If you are around Dave long enough, he will eventually make some idiomatic response that fairly shouts *West Virginia*. Just the other day, for example, I had been talking—possibly at some length—which prompted Dave to complain that I was "making more racket than a jack-ass in a tin barn." Then there was the time he provided a description of the color red that was so vivid it has yet to be surpassed by anything I've ever heard, before or since. I have forgotten the particular item of interest; whatever it was, Dave said it was "redder than a fox's ass during pokeberry season."

West Virginia has expanding pockets of urbanity, there is no doubt about it: art galleries, theaters, museums, universities—that sort of thing; but an undercurrent of folk culture tenaciously persists. Travel around the state and you can't miss it. Like the sign posted outside the entrance to the country store Dave and I stopped at just outside Durbin that read: "Please don't spit in front of door or near door." Or, the Annual Roadkill Cook-off we wandered into while passing through Marlinton on our way to fish the Elk River. You can't grow up in culture like that without its having an effect on you, which may be why Dave was so disappointed that we didn't stick around to see what was on the roadkill menu.

The reason I gave Dave the post had to do with his customary way of interacting with strangers. In his case, he knows none.

Bill and Dave and I frequently travel together on one trip or another, and when we do, Bill and I hope to make as few stops as possible. We know that when we do stop, for whatever reason, we will be there for a while.

Dave talks to whoever happens to be around. It could be a waitress at a restaurant, the receptionist at a visitor center, the clerk behind the counter at a sandwich shop, people at yard sales—where Dave searches for antique fishing lures to add to his nationally recognized collection—or some guys hanging around a convenience store where we have stopped for coffee and gas.

He will talk to anyone, and it won't be superficial, hi-how-are-you conversation, either. We are talking length. Bill and I often wonder how many hours we have spent leaning against walls while Dave finished a conversation with his newest best friend.

We can't even stop for a quick pee. Bill and I will take care of business, zip up, wash our hands, and hustle back to the truck, eager to get on the road again…only to notice that Dave is missing. Always a bad sign.

There was even the occasion when we were stopped for road construction and Dave got involved in deep conversation with the person manning the stop sign. By the time the signal came to let the traffic through, we had learned that the attendant had just moved back in state after being away for several years; what he had been doing while away; and more information about his family than seemed possible in the time our line of traffic had been stopped.

Particularly if it's West Virginia we happen to be traveling through, it is uncanny how Dave will get around to knowing someone who is nephew or second cousin or some distant kin third removed of the person he's talking to.

Frankly, I don't know how he does it. But he clearly has a gift, an extraordinary gift. Whenever I try that kind of friendliness with strangers, they usually end up looking at me through suspicious eyes and moving away, as though they expect me to ask them for money or hand them a religious tract. But Dave pulls it off, every time.

Bill and I endure these performances—sometimes mildly irritated because we would like to get to wherever it is we are going, but mostly we watch with head-shaking fascination. "I swear, he'll talk to a damn post," Bill said one day as the two of us looked on, shifting from foot to foot as we thought about the fishing we weren't doing. When I gave Dave the post, it needed no explanation.

Dave and I met in 1975. I had come to Bedford, Virginia, that year to be the rector of St. John's Episcopal Church. Dave arrived in 1967, to open an optometry practice. A mutual friend who knew I was interested in fishing introduced us, and we have been good friends since, even throughout my twenty-seven-year absence, before I retired and returned to central Virginia in the spring of 2008.

It was a wonder that our friendship took as quickly and as solidly as it did, given the particulars of our first fishing trip together.

At the time, Dave was already an accomplished bass fisherman. He had grown up fishing, and along with Jim, his childhood friend, enjoyed a Tom Sawyer kind of childhood. (I later learned a lot about what those two got up to in their growing-up years, but reputations are at stake so I'll stick with the fishing.)

They caught hellgrammites and lizards and fished for smallmouth bass in the Greenbrier River. They caught trout in Howard's Creek and Anthony's Creek, and largemouth in farm ponds spread around Greenbrier County.

When Dave moved to Memphis for optometry school, he would drive seventy miles to Horseshoe Lake, Arkansas, where he would rent a boat and hone his skills fishing for bass with plastic worms, spinner baits, and an assortment of balsa-wood lures that imitated baitfish and frogs.

By the time he opened his optometry practice, he had skills that only improved as he applied them on Smith Mountain Lake, the James and Maury rivers, and a multitude of farm ponds owned by patients who came through his office. Dave had permission to fish so many ponds, I wondered if there was a place on the intake form asking patients to indicate any fishable water they had on their land. He also started fishing tournaments, and won a few.

At the time we made plans to get together, Dave was considered one of the best fishermen in the area. His office walls were lined with citations from the fish and game commission, and taxidermy mounts of trophy fish: largemouth, smallmouth, three species of trout, and an open-jawed muskie with menacing teeth. To this collection, a state-record rainbow trout would later be added.

In contrast, except for a few widely separated occasions, I had not fished in nearly a dozen years: through college, seminary, and my first church job in Richmond, Virginia. I can remember a day trip with a seminary classmate to fish for striped bass in the Chesapeake Bay, and some perch fishing on Lake Erie while I was a counselor at a summer camp, but not much more.

Before that, I had fished for trout with my grandfather, caught bass and bream in a few ponds, and done a little saltwater pier fishing with my father on summer vacations. Not much of a resume compared with Dave's.

Dave picked me up after work and we drove to a pond owned by an apple farmer who was a friend of Dave's and a parishioner of mine. Dave went right to work, casting plastic worms around the branches of a fallen tree that lay half submerged along a steep bank at the pond's deepest end.

I scarcely knew how to begin. My rod was old, and my reel was stiff from lack of use. I had none of the right lures. I hadn't even dressed properly.

By the time darkness set in, I had: upended my tackle box, forcing me to grope on hands and knees in the tall grass to recover its contents; spent the remnants of the evening shivering because I had worn only a T-shirt and had not anticipated how much the temperature would fall after the sun dropped below the ridgeline; and caught no fish.

Dave, on the other hand, had done quite well. Among the bass he caught was one that topped five pounds and another that exceeded four. And in his long-sleeve shirt and jacket, he had been quite comfortable doing so.

That was more than thirty years ago. Since then, I have become a better fisherman; still not Dave's equal, which is not likely to happen given the instincts he's developed from an early head start, but at least I can hold my own. And it only took that one chilly evening for me to learn how to dress.

Over the past three decades, we have fished every month of the year in all manner of conditions: subfreezing cold, rain, wind, snow, and withering summer heat. On a trip we took in January of 1998, just after El Niño, the water was so high people thought we were crazy. But we had the Watauga virtually to ourselves—not to mention all the fish we caught.

We have hired guides, explored on our own, and traveled to destinations far from home. I can still see Dave greeting me in the airport in Bozeman, Montana, where he had come to fish for a week while I was there on a sabbatical leave…coming toward me carrying his rods and bags, and wearing the Mickey Mouse ears a cooperative flight attendant had provided when he left the plane.

We have sat around hundreds of campfires and spent weeks on the ground sleeping in tents. Now in our sixties, we remember with fond smiles the time—it was 1993—we sat next to our campfire and watched two very attractive women in the campsite next to us undress. It was dark, and their lantern silhouetted them against the walls of their tent…quite distinct silhouettes they were. It was like when we were children and pantomimed behind a backlit sheet. I know, this may not seem particularly titillating now, but after a week in the woods it had its effect. We still refer to the occasion as "the evening of the light show."

We have rented mice-infested cabins, hiked through woods and fields, and traveled thousands of miles on mountain roads. We have spent hours tying flies, picking morels, and driving to one river or another—eating a mountain of unhealthy food along the way. We've had days when we caught fish till our arms ached, and others when we went home without a strike. But whatever the circumstances, we always seemed to salvage a good time and to render the day well-spent.

One spring we made a much anticipated trip to several of the storied streams of the Catskill Mountains: the east and west branches of the Delaware, the Willowemoc, and the Beaverkill. It was a late spring that year, and we had arrived too early. The water temperature was still in the forties, and nothing was happening. Those who lived in the area and knew the water well were biding their time indoors; they definitely weren't fishing.

For four days Dave and I flailed the water. We tried every trick we knew and caught nothing. But still we talk about that trip: the people we met, the rivers we fished, the towns we visited, and the laughs we had. We even consider going back sometime, when the water's warm and the bugs are on.

There are some who know both of us who wonder what has made this friendship last so long, because to them we seem so unlike in style and temperament. They assume that fishing must be the bond. But they are wrong.

They note our differences that seem obvious and contradictory, such as Dave's relation to organized religion—the church—which is remote at best, while I made a career of it. Dave, they observe, is laid-back and spontaneous, and I am not.

I once had a parishioner whose motto was: Life's too short to wake up without a smile on your face—which could just as well be said of Dave. But certainly not of me, especially when I settle into one of my introspective moods.

Dave is khakis and blue jeans. I am suits and wingtip shoes (that is, until I retired; now I wear mostly khakis and blue jeans).

I once asked Dave how often he wore a jacket and tie. He said that depended on how often someone died or got married. He corrected himself, though, when he remembered The Gobbler Club.

Dave is one of the founders of The Gobbler Club, of which there are roughly fifty members. Initiates are admitted only when an old member dies, resigns, or moves away. It is very exclusive.

The Gobbler Club meets four times a year—coat and tie required—for the purpose of fellowship and the eating of turkey testicles. You may not even be aware that turkeys have testicles, but they do. At least the males do. You can look it up if you don't believe me.

Dave took me as a guest once, so I speak from experience. The properly dressed members (all male, if that's a surprise) and their guests gather in the dining hall at the Elks National Home in Bedford. The evening begins with fellowship over drinks. This lasts for…well, long enough to put one in the mood for eating turkey nuts.

After cocktails, the group repairs to a long banquet table for a feast of black-eyed peas, stewed tomatoes, corn bread, and the *piece de resistance*—fried. There are so many turkey farms just north of Bedford that a fresh and ample supply is never a problem.

Following dinner and dessert, joke- and story-telling time begins, and that rounds out the evening. The Gobbler Club is a revered institution in Bedford County, with a venerable reputation. I still regret that I missed becoming a charter member when I moved to North Carolina.

Anyway, you can see why Dave would need a jacket and tie at least four times a year.

Truth is, Dave and I are kindred spirits, however incongruous our friendship may appear to others. Dave may not warm a church pew, but he has values that any faith community would applaud. His Lions Club chapter gave him its highest award, and the hospital honored him with a distinguished community service award. And he and his wife, Beth, raised two terrific children who are well on their way to becoming responsible, productive citizens in the communities in which they now live.

Dave might not share my interest in writing and books, but he has an impressive collection of finely crafted bamboo rods. And behind his unprepossessing, occasionally tobacco-chewing demeanor, he's got as much insight and wisdom as any Ph.D. I know. I would liken our friendship to a good Kentucky bourbon that had to age and mellow to reach the quality it has achieved.

I once heard a linguist speak on what's happening to the English language. The part that really interested me was his observations on how we cheapen words. Like a lot of products that have become inferior imitations of the original version, we seem to be doing much the same thing with speech.

Now even a trip to the mall can be *"awesome!"* and athletes are referred to as "heroes." I'll add my two cents and suggest that it's all part of our high-drama culture of excess wherein we pass out trophies for merely showing up, and give a standing ovation—now meaningless—for the most lackluster performance.

That is why it bugged the hell out of me when some guy I hardly knew kept referring to me as "friend." He probably meant well, like the teller at the bank who tells me—and every other customer who passes her window—to have a nice day.

Still, when I heard him call me friend for about the fourth time, it was all I could do to keep my mouth shut. When you have a friend, a friend worthy of the designation, you just hate to see the word tossed around like that.

In any case, Dave and I are friends.

FROM GENERATION TO GENERATION

An article in this morning's paper reported that the Chesapeake Bay is in big trouble. The problem continues to be pollutants. One official warned that if we don't get moving with a serious cleanup effort it soon might be too late to bother.

There is a long history of official pronouncements setting deadlines for improvement. But deadlines keep getting moved forward, and deterioration of the nation's largest estuary continues apace.

When I was a boy of five, and my father was stationed at Langley Air Force Base, the two of us spent many a pleasant evening together fishing the bay for spot, croaker, and flounder. Dad would buy a half-pound of shrimp and a couple dozen minnows, and we would drive to Old Point Comfort and cast our baited lines from the edge of the massive creosote-stained dock as we watched the ferries come and go. At other times, we would tie a chicken neck to the crab trap Dad had built, and carry our scrabbling, claw-wielding catch home in a bushel basket to steam in a boiling pot.

Those idyllic days are among my favorite memories. But their circumstances aren't repeatable. The Chesapeake Bay Bridge-Tunnel eliminated the need for the ferries, and the landing pier at Old Point Comfort was taken down and carried away years ago. And who knows what fishing will be like in the bay's shaky and uncertain future.

While it is distressing to contemplate the possibility, the Chesapeake Bay may be no more than a bellwether for a dismal time when parents and their children will have fewer opportunities to deepen their intimacy with nature. Fishing—along with hunting, camping, canoeing, hiking, birding, and other outdoor activities done with someone else—has been for many of us the vehicle through which we forged enduring bonds of mutual affection. I can't help wondering what the consequences will be when such activities—now threatened—become less available to us and to our children and grandchildren.

My buddies and I fish many of the rivers and streams that eventually make their way to the Chesapeake, and evidence is abundant that the bay's problem is a systemic one that begins hundreds of miles upstream. A series of fish kills has demonstrated serious damage in the Shenandoah, and ugly lesions are showing up on bass taken near the headwaters of the James. Even on the smallest mountain streams, dollops of phosphate foam float on backwater eddies like whipped froth on a cup of fancy gourmet coffee.

The hard part is accepting my own role in this abuse. Much of the junk that contaminates our waterways comes from lawns like mine—from the fertilizer and weed killer I apply to keep it looking sharp. Recently, I hired a professional lawn care service to do those chores for me. It guarantees results; its applications will be more frequent and, no doubt, more potent.

As consequential as it is, though, pollution isn't the only reason a father and his son (or daughter) have fewer opportunities to pick up their rods and head off for an afternoon of bonding on a nearby stream. Increasingly, the obstacle is the lack of streams available *to* fish, at least those that don't require a club membership or a hefty access fee.

Dave often tells of growing up in Lewisburg, West Virginia, at a time when he could fish just about anywhere he wanted. "Nobody minded," he said. "As long as you closed the gates and didn't cause any problems, you could cross their land to get to the river, or stop and fish in one of their ponds."

Those days are gone. Posted signs are now as prevalent as stoplights. And much of the water that used to be open to the public has been acquired by private interests.

After I moved to North Carolina in 1981, I made frequent trips to the mountains west of our High Point home. It was well worth the two-hour drive. Friends and I would fish long stretches of the Watauga River near Foscoe, and the Elk near the town of Banner Elk. Today, much of the water we used to fish along the Watauga is lined with vacation homes and planned communities. Unless you live there, fishing is no longer allowed.

Access to areas adjacent to the Elk is even more restricted. A fishing guide once told me: "I wouldn't mess with the Elk; you'd be lucky to find fifty feet that isn't posted." Throughout the last ten years I lived in North Carolina, I did most of my fishing in eastern Tennessee.

On several occasions, through the kindness of a friend, I was given permission to fish a privately owned section of the Linville River that is reserved for members and their guests. It is very exclusive, patrolled, and those caught trespassing are prosecuted.

One afternoon I ran into two boys—brothers, thirteen to fifteen years old—whose heavy mountain accents assured me they were native to the area. They were standing on the bank with their hands jammed in their pockets, looking at the water. We chatted for a few minutes, and one of them—pointing to a sturdy oak that leaned out over a bend in the river—told me their grandfather had once caught an eight-pound brown in the pool beneath. Before it had become private water, that is.

The boys also told me about the time they had tried to fish the river and been arrested and fined for trespassing. They were neither angry nor bitter about the incident—more like incredulous. "I don't know why they's upset," the one boy drawled. "We was fishin' at night." I took their response as ingenuous and innocent. What should be expected from two unsophisticated mountain boys whose kin had fished the river for generations and who now are told that it's off-limits—even at night, when you aren't even disturbing anyone? I didn't ask if their grandfather was still alive, but I left feeling sad that here was one more place they couldn't fish with him, even if he were.

Before this lament turns into a self-righteous screed, let me acknowledge the complications. I have seen the trash some "sportsmen" leave behind, and heard the outrage of farmers and landowners whose livestock and property have been damaged. I get it why they post their land.

The fishing guide I referred to earlier carries a large plastic trash bag with him on his guiding trips. I watched one morning as he filled it full with bottles, cans, cups, and other castoff items that had accumulated around the launching ramp. He did this in full view of a half-dozen other anglers.

"I do this every morning before we take off," he said. "I don't know if it does any good; I just hope someone might notice and stop contributing to the mess."

There is a lot of mess everywhere, and more of us are contributing to it since the days I fished the Chesapeake Bay with my dad. The population has nearly doubled, and more of us are crowded into cities and suburbs, having abandoned the farms and rural areas once inhabited by our forebears. Power plants, gas refineries, and factories are required to sustain us. There is no simple solution here, and I have none to offer.

Yet, I continue to wonder what happens when our connection to nature—to water, wildlife, and the good earth—becomes estranged and remote. Surely we will lose some essential piece of the human soul, fracture the intimate bond we share with all living things—the bond that defines our discreet role in the intricate and complex web of God's creation.

Most of the guys in our group are grandfathers. We often talk about the old days and fret about what the fishing is going to be like for our grandkids, if there is to be any at all.

We don't come up with much in the way of solutions. We usually end up bitching about everything that's wrong instead—pollution, too many people, greedy corporations, careless developers, too much private water. We have a long list, and you don't want to get us started.

We say we don't really know what to do about it. I have heard myself make that excuse on any number of occasions. It's a lot easier, you know, to point fingers at the other culprits. Otherwise, I might have to reconsider that lawn care service, and maybe even be willing to put up with a few more weeds growing in my yard.

I better stop right here. You never know where thoughts like that might lead.

Time Passing

Having just returned from our fall gathering, I am more preoccupied than usual with the swiftness of time and the consequent changes left in the wake of its ineluctable passing. There are ample reasons for my melancholic musings. Foremost is John's recent birthday, a milestone of sorts for our group's collective identity: there is no one left who is still under sixty. And George, our oldest member, I was reminded, will soon turn seventy-seven.

There was more gallows humor this time about "the last man standing." And when we talked about what to do with the money that has accumulated in the kitty from our annual fall auction, someone joked that we needed to save it to buy more benches—referring to the bench we purchased in honor of Ed, the first and only member of our group to have died. We all laughed, in a subdued and forced kind of way, I thought.

Home now, after four days with the boys, I take a long, hard look at the eight-by-thirteen picture that hangs on my office wall. Most of the time, I hardly register its presence, even though I pass it nearly every day. It decorates the room, along with sundry other pictures, diplomas, and mementos, seldom more noticeable than paint. But this time, before sitting down to write, I let my eyes linger over the posed scene of us standing shoulder to shoulder as we await the shutter click that will capture this brief moment, this visible reminder of what we once were, before time hurried us along, reminding us that there is no pausing along our journey to the final cast.

I check, but no date is penned on the back to specify when it was taken. Somewhere around twenty-five years ago is my best guess. From the way we all look, that can't be far off.

Who are these men? I recognize them, but the changes we have undergone are strikingly evident in the contrast between the color photograph before me and the image in my brain of our recent trip. *Can this really be us?*

To the man, we are thicker. Our centers of gravity have slipped a notch, or maybe two. No one is lean and angular anymore. Our bulk, once a demarcation of muscle and strength, has migrated to less comely—and less healthy—stations along our expanding frames. There are more gray hairs and gray beards, despite the paradox of there being significantly less hair in general than there was twenty years ago. But let's not belabor the comparison. No doubt you get the picture as well as I do as I stand here studying the images of us framed on my office wall.

At the risk of sounding too philosophical, this hard evidence of time's passing does seem to pose certain existential questions that beg attention. Foremost is the point at which getting older qualifies one for the designation *old.* Surely there is more involved in the computation than numbers piling up along the continuum of chronological age.

After all, it appears to be a well-established fact that how we view ourselves has more than a little to do with how we behave and interact with others. It's the self-image thing. (In our culture, where narcissism is a practiced virtue, I doubt that needs explaining.) Every motivational book I have ever read eventually boiled down to one salient prescription: that one achieves or succeeds based on the *belief* that one can. Or its obverse: that one fails because one does *not* believe sufficiently that one can succeed and achieve.

And when my friends and I finally accept the designation that we are "old"...old fishermen, old men...I fear that self-defining, and self-limiting, description may generate its own brand of restricting behavioral responses.

To put it another way: believing you are old causes you to act the way an old person is "supposed" to act; and by acting the way an old person is supposed to act, you convince yourself and others that the inherent limitations of your newly assigned status are well-prescribed. And round and round it goes until you stop doing what you very well might be capable of doing, merely because common (mis)perception says you can't...or aren't supposed to.

Health and ability obviously impose realistic limits on all of us. And there are too many examples of seniors who have attempted to foolishly surpass reasonable competencies, as anyone who has had to argue with a feeble parent that it is time to stop driving well knows. Or—less lethal but no less troublesome—is the pathetic old fart who still believes he is Lothario and fetches after women half his age. Yet, much of societal pigeonholing—whether of gender, race, religion, nationality, age, or some other identifiable niche—is propaganda, and it is time we get past it.

Well, now I have gotten that off my chest, and you know where I am coming from. Looking at this twenty-five-year-old picture has stirred up some feisty sentiments. But let us move along.

As far as acting like stereotypical old guys, the boys and I aren't there yet. And I have the facts to prove it. Still, if I am to justify this bold conclusion, I'll have to present an objective argument.

To that end, I have constructed my own classification system for measuring vitality, a five-factor set of criteria for comparing functional age with the less-revealing status of chronology alone, five keys to determining if you are still getting the best out of life.

Quibble over one or more of the choices if you must, but it seems to me that if you have these basics covered your life can't be too bad, not too bad at all. But you be the judge. Here they are: meaning and purpose; health; companionship; sex; and physical activity.

Let's begin with health. All the men in our group have their particular aches and pains, or one kind of chronic condition or another, but all seem to manage. Dave has a pesky back problem, my hip bothered me on this recent trip, about half the group is on blood pressure or cholesterol medication, and John has bad hair, which he really needs to do something about. There are some mornings when it is too disobedient to be out in public, much less at the breakfast table. We have tried to tell him that on numerous occasions, so far to no effect.

We are definitely sentient testimonials to better living through chemistry. I see a lot of those multi-lid medication dispensers with the individualized compartments poking out of shaving kits when I visit the head. And the hand-to-mouth pill pop between sips of morning coffee is so routine an observer might think he was witnessing a form of geriatric tai chi.

George and John definitely lead in pill and capsule consumption. George comes to breakfast listing to one side from a fistful of multicolored, multi-shaped conduits of nutrients and prescription drugs. Somehow he manages to get through the lot by the end of the meal. But it takes awhile.

John invariably dumps his load on the table next to his plate, which is how I came to count them one morning—quite surreptitiously, so I wouldn't be noticed and accused of perverse curiosity. Nonchalantly, feigning preoccupation with deep thoughts, I strolled past John's chair, cutting my eyes in quick darts of fact-finding glimpses until I was sure I had it right. There were thirteen. Thirteen rounded gel caps, oblong capsules, and little solid circles and squares—an impressive array. Mostly vitamins, I was to learn. John's wife, Phyllis, is really into foods and nutrition, which explained a lot. I concluded that when you're married to an attractive woman who is ten years your junior, there is real incentive to keep yourself up—no pun intended.

John dutifully choked down his pile each morning; not one word of complaint. What's more, he seems healthy and happy enough, judging from the way he greets each new day singing like a lunatic.

We may need some biochemical assistance in confronting the customary and expected attritions of passing years, but there isn't one in our group who can't reap full enjoyment out of the activities he pursues. And while I might fairly be accused of bragging on the boys, I like to think that it's this grateful attitude that is the most determining component of our general state of health.

Companionship is next, the indicator that reveals social connections and the presence of supportive friends and relationships.

It seems too obvious a point to make that our group exists for companionship. We have been fishing and hanging out for more than thirty years, longer than the average married couple has been together. And like most long-term relationships, there were certain issues that had to be "worked through" if we were to continue being friends.

Camping and fishing may be enough to draw a group of men together, but it won't be enough to sustain them over several decades if they don't find other reasons to hang in there once they discover their disparate attitudes and beliefs—which our group has in abundance.

There was a time when I thought politics might bring an end to us. We are about evenly divided on political philosophy—half Republican, half Democrat, much like the nation in that regard. Our passions run from one end of the political continuum to the other, with Jim and me being the most polar opposite. Jim is a zealous conservative, and I'm a progressive. Oh, let's not mince words here: I'm an unabashed liberal, and just as convinced of the rectitude of my positions as Jim is of his. That's the problem.

When we first learned we had strong and conflicting views about matters political, there were disagreements, then arguments that escalated into interchanges that traveled too close to insult, the sort of thing that can bring a friendship down.

It may be that each of us decided we weren't getting anywhere banging each other's ears with our favored version of good governance, but I like to think it was growing maturity that enabled us to eventually accept and look beyond each other's politics and find those deeper connections upon which lasting friendships are built.

Two years ago, my father needed some highly specialized brain surgery that required technology and medical expertise not available in Lynchburg, where he lives in a retirement community with my mother. His doctor referred him to the medical center at the University of Virginia—a teaching hospital—that had both the equipment and expertise needed for Dad's unique procedure.

Jim and his wife, Nancy, live in Charlottesville, only a few miles from the hospital. When they learned I would be with Dad throughout his hospitalization, and needed to stay in town for a couple of days, they invited me to their home. It was a generous offer. They fed me, provided a room, and cheered me up with drink and good conversation after my long days at the hospital. As I remember, we never talked about politics, which is just as well. But we did enjoy each other's company, and I left feeling grateful for their practical assistance and genuine concern, even if they are Republicans.

It used to surprise me when some old politician died—one reputed for a strong ideological bent—and a colleague of opposite persuasion would lament his passing with tears in his eyes as he spoke persuasively of their long and valued friendship. After all these years of bantering with Jim, I no longer have difficulty understanding how or why such things occur.

I could very well be wrong, but I have worked with people all my professional life (that's what clergy do), and based on my own experience, nothing more, I'll make the claim that more men talk about having good friends than actually do. They may have a cadre of acquaintances, but, sad to say, aren't even able to recognize the difference between those and friends.

There was a clinical study—from a distinguished source, as I recall—that indicated solid, dependable, authentic, straight-talking relationships contribute to longevity. I might be reluctant to tell my buddies this (there are some things guys just don't do), but my life would be much diminished without them, and they have been an invaluable presence in my life on more than a few occasions, even when they didn't know it.

There are a lot of names we call one another, especially when we've had a few drinks and get to horsing around. Most aren't fit to print. The most accurate—despite the irony of being the one least heard—the one I suspect we all value most and, moreover, feel the most… is friend.

Because this book is a memoir about a group of men, a five-category inventory of vitality could hardly leave out sex. Granted, we may not approach the subject with the same intensity we did thirty or twenty or even ten years ago, but the topic is still a top-five pick.

I think all the boys agree with Dave's assessment of our current status. Drawing on his vast repertoire of aphorisms and folk wisdom, when the matter of sex recently inserted itself into our cocktail hour conversation, he made a summary statement so profound in its simplicity, so says-it-all in its descriptive analysis, that we could only nod in thoughtful agreement, impressed that Dave could put into one succinct sentence what we all were thinking.

The subject of sex usually comes up when…actually, I can't say there is a "usually"; it just comes up. That is one thing that hasn't changed over the years. We will be talking, and the first thing you know we are discussing sex. I sometimes wonder if women do this when they get together. I have asked a few women I know, but they just smile tolerantly and shake their heads, sometimes accompanied by eye rolling. Still, there is something about the gesture that leaves me unconvinced.

Anyway, when sex is the subject, Dave will sit back in his chair and listen while the rest of us hold forth on some specific provocation, such as a recent urological exam. Then he'll clear his throat, rearrange his wad of chew, and await our undivided attention: "You know, boys, I look at it this way: I might not be as good as I once was, but I am as good once as I always was." Which is followed by head bobbing and general agreement all around.

We have heard this line from Dave before, and we know what's coming, but there is something affirming about repetition, like when children want to hear the same bedtime story until they know the thing by heart. We are always pleased when Dave repeats himself. His words are so comforting and reassuring.

There was one vignette from our last trip that speaks volumes on how the boys are faring on the vitality scale at this point. We held the annual silent auction again, the one we hold every fall, when each of us brings items for the others to bid on. Over the years that has included anything from nifty fishing gear to crap that didn't sell at someone's yard sale.

Jim was back this year with several packets of Cialis, which he claimed was a seventy-five-dollar value. Having no personal need for a synthetic aid, and therefore no purchasing experience, I was unable to comment on whether the price was inflated.

Jim added consumer appeal by announcing that this would be the last year for the offer. He had been getting his supply from his son-in-law, a pharmaceutical rep, who had recently started peddling another drug. There will be no more free samples of Cialis. Our group expressed its sympathies and hoped the loss would not lead to any marital discord for Jim, who has been married to his Nancy for more than forty years.

At last year's auction, John was the bidder not to be denied, which was understandable given that he had remarried just months before. This year the bidding was noticeably more subdued, which I attribute to the state of the national economy. It certainly could not have had anything to do with the capabilities of the bidders: let me make that perfectly clear.

After time was called, and the sheets of paper beside each item were tallied, it was announced that George had submitted the highest bid—which was nowhere near seventy-five dollars. Not even halfway close. Whatever the reason, George got the pills at a bargain price, a real steal, and I don't think Jim was very happy about it. He looked a little agitated, and I thought I heard him mumble something about how he should have kept them for himself, but I can't be certain. And before I forget, did I mention that George will be seventy-eight on his next birthday?

Let's move along to the fourth category: physical activity.

The golf clubs showed up again this trip. It is beginning to look like they will be a permanent presence, despite strong objections. Several of us consider it a sorry state of affairs, given that our original stated purpose was to be a fishing group.

It is a curious observation—from a purely sociological point of view—that it was the Republicans among us who introduced golf into our group life. Now we are *really* a house divided.

A couple of the golfers did bring their fly rods along on this last trip, feigning continued interest in our original purpose, but they fooled no one. Not one of their rods ever left its protective case.

Yet, while the golfers leave for the links as the rest of us depart for the water, we all regroup in the early evening for drinks before dinner and have about as good a time as any group of men could hope to. The recreational divide hasn't affected our camaraderie any more than the political split has fractured any friendships or caused a decline in mutual respect. Nation, take note.

Whether it's golf or fishing, the boys remain active. This year a new activity was added by four of the fishermen. Dave, Bill, John, and I bought used mountain bikes that we tricked out for fly-fishing. We brought them along, strapped to a carrying rack, and used them to travel to and from the water.

It was great fun, and practical as hell. The day we fished the special regulation area of the Jackson River, we unloaded the two-wheelers in the parking lot at the lower end of Hidden Valley and tied our rods and gear to the frames. We mounted up and pedaled three miles along the path that leads upriver, stashed the bikes in a clump of trees, and agreed on a time to get back together before we split up to fish different sections of the river. When the appointed hour arrived, we reclaimed the bikes and cycled out.

We bumped over rocks and splashed through mudholes formed by a recent rain, and one of us wrecked trying to ride through a tributary stream that cut across our path. We arrived at the parking lot winded, sweaty, and splattered with mud. It was an exhilarating ride, making us feel like boys again, not to mention making the trip back to the truck in a fraction of the time it would have taken had we walked. Not bad for a group of guys who are all over sixty.

The boys and I are aware that the time for doing such things is limited. And who knows how long that will be. Then again, does anyone, of any age? For now, we are enjoying the ride…including the bikes. We have already decided to bring them next trip; they may even become permanent. It's a whole new group concept, we realize, and involves an additional item on the checklist of things we have to pack; but bikes are a lot more appropriate than golf clubs, even if the putting bastards have accused us of trying to start a cycling club.

The final item on the vitality measuring scale is meaning and purpose. This may be, and probably is, the most important of the five. Everyone needs a purpose in life, a reason to get up in the morning; it's essential.

That point having been made, I see no need for a lengthy explanation on how the boys are doing with the "purpose in life" critique. We already have our next trip planned. What more needs to be said?

DINING OUT

Whenever he returns from one of our semiannual four-day trips, John claims his weight is up by at least ten pounds. I don't doubt it. Most of his gain comes from the amount of food he puts away: his dinner plate looks like the commingling of an entire Thanksgiving meal—for six. But much of his gain—along with the poundage larded onto the rest of us—comes from what we eat while we are roughing it in the woods.

Jim has been our camp cook from the beginning, and he is superb. Going back to the early days, when we hiked into the Cranberry Backcountry, carrying our equipment on our backs, Jim has put together menus that a first-class restaurant couldn't match.

Throughout those early years, he had to do the cooking under circumstances that would have caused most chefs to turn in their spatulas. Much of it was done over the glowing coals of an open fire, dodging smoke and making allowances for the possibility of rain.

The time we camped along Red Run, it rained so hard the mud was up to our ankles as we stood under a dripping plastic tarp eating off metal plates. It reminded me of feeding time at the dairy farm where I worked as a college student—all of us huddled together with our faces in our plates, gobbling our food, our shifting feet making sucking noises in the soupy mud. It was all very bovine. The only thing missing was the mooing, although the gulping noises from our frenzied eating rendered a reasonable impersonation.

To help with the cooking, especially when it rained, we fashioned a crude oven from stones, a thick square of metal sheeting, and a three-foot section of galvanized pipe. It was a bear carrying the metal slab and the pipe to the campsite for the first time, but we dealt with any future inconvenience by stashing the components in a shallow mountain cave between trips.

We called the contraption Baal, after the ancient Canaanite god mentioned in the Old Testament. The name seemed most fitting. Perched on its supporting rocks, nestled in burning coals, its slanting pipe puffing out pods of smoke, it looked like an apparatus designed for some sacrificial rite. Besides, I was pleased to show off the particulars of my theological education.

After we stopped camping and transitioned to the lodge, we had a full kitchen at our disposal. This made the task of cooking much easier for Jim, and the ritual of cleaning up easier for the rest of us. Unless you've had to boil river water in a pot to wash your dishes, you really can't appreciate the full blessings of running water, a sink, and—glory be!—a dishwasher. Meals and cleaning up take a lot less time and energy these days, a good thing because we don't have as much.

Now we even have a dining room, with a long boardinghouse table at which we sit, politely, with napkins in our laps. That's a distinct contrast to the meal we had one fall on the Cranberry when the temperature fell into the teens and snow streaked vertically across our faces as we tucked down inside our parkas and ate like cavemen, leaning into the fire. While that may have been our coldest trip, there were others when we were able to ice our whiskey with the rain that had frozen on the tarp.

There are a few aspects of eating outside that we miss. I emphasize *few*. Occasionally, one of the boys will drift into a nostalgic mood and suggest that we go camping one more time; "just for old time's sake" is the predictable refrain. It won't happen. The comment is usually made within our warm, dry lodge, and the proponent has forgotten how addicted we have become to such luxuries.

Some of what we miss, or so we say, are the foods harvested by our own hands. I am going to guess this has more to do with a primitive hunter/gatherer instinct than it does with the taste of whatever it was we used to carry back to camp. It may be related to that lingering belief men cling to, that warrior fantasy that convinces us we could kick Superman's ass, if we really had to.

When we camped along the Cranberry in early spring, a pungent member of the garlic family known as ramps grew wild in the mountains of West Virginia. We had no sooner set up camp than John would be off, shovel in hand, in search of a patch.

Ramp eating is a popular custom in the mountain communities where they grow. You may even stumble on a Ramp Festival if you happen to be up that way in the early spring. The one thing to remember if you find yourself at an event where ramps are on the menu is this: when one person eats them, everyone else had better eat them, too, not out of preference, but definitely in self-defense.

There is something about the digestive processing of ramps that gives them their notorious distinction. It's the way they exit through the pores and transform breath into a lethal weapon. Ramps are similar to garlic and onions, but exponentially more muscular. To compare them would be like placing a flame next to a volcano. If others in your company are eating ramps, the only antidote to near asphyxiation is to eat them yourself. Apparently clashing sulfuric forces cancel each other out.

Ramps were allowed on our camp menu for only a brief period. Some of us who had never tried them were curious. In my case, since I was a seminary student during the height of the sixties, it may have been a delayed adolescent desire to experiment with a body-altering substance that prompted me to partake. But the need was quickly satisfied. After the serving pot had been passed around and we had all ingested the green weed a time or two, enough of us said *No more.* Thereafter, ramps became a controlled substance, their use restricted.

Perhaps in the future, if he proves some medicinal need, John can get a use permit. Meanwhile, if we catch him with any more ramp stash he's going to get busted.

During that phase when we camped along the Jackson River in Virginia, thick mats of watercress grew in a spring that seeped from a rocky cliff behind our camp. We mixed the watercress in our salads, and the water we drank straight from the bowl-shaped indentation below the rock from which it leaked, clear as air and cold as arctic ice.

It is probably fortunate that none of us contracted giardia, but the water had to pass through long corridors of porous rock before it got to us, so we took the chance.

It was worth it. Seldom have I tasted water so sweet and so pure.

There is an aristocratic mushroom that shows itself in the early spring. Known as a morel, it grows in wood-ed mountains, often near the ridgelines, and is well-dispersed. Seldom are more than a few found in close proximity, and with its brown spongy top, it is well-disguised among the fallen leaves. Those who harvest morels—by hand only—must concentrate and meticulously observe the ground over which they search.

All of this contributes to the morel's exclusive repu-tation. Mostly, though, it's the delicate, woodsy taste that endears it to gourmets and fine restaurants, which are willing to pay handsomely to include it on their menus.

There was a day when we used to take time from our fishing to look for morels. It started when a friend told us about a place where they were known to grow. This had to be a good friend, because morel lovers ordinarily keep such valued knowledge to themselves.

We put the trucks in four-wheel drive and lumbered up an old logging road that ended a few hundred yards from where we had been advised to search. Fanning out in a line, plastic bags in hand, heads bent to the ground, eyes roving back and forth in defined arcs, we hunted for the wrinkled conical caps hiding shyly among the leaves and sticks and decaying flora that lay atop the mottled forest floor.

There were times when the combined haul was suf-ficient for Jim to bread and bake them on a large cookie sheet to serve as a side dish on their own. When the pick-ing was less productive, he cut them into sections and made them the highlight of a salad. However we ate them, we savored every lingering bite.

They are still out there, waiting each spring to be discovered. Maybe the time will come when our group will combine memory with initiative, and we will search for them again. It has been awhile, and I sure do miss them.

Two of the boys, Wayne and George—both from West Virginia, which may have some bearing on what follows—at one time had a strong appetite for a canned meat known as Banner Sausage. I don't know if it is still around, but back then the two of them bitched like a first-base coach disputing a close call if Jim didn't include a can in our groceries.

When oozed out of its cylinder, sliced in half-inch-thick circles, and fried in a skillet, it vaguely resembled sausage patties. George and Wayne considered it the ideal complement for breakfast eggs and toast. The rest of us disagreed. We tried it once, and once was enough, quite enough.

How George and Wayne got started on the stuff in the first place I still can't comprehend, but, like two addicts, they wouldn't give it up. So Banner Sausage became a matter of friendly contention: George and Wayne advocating for inclusion; the rest of us countering that we'd rather eat our socks.

Taste, however, is subjective, and it's hard to determine whether something is good eatin' until you have put the matter to a scientific test. It was Jim who came up with the protocol.

Before our upcoming trip, he bought the requested Banner Sausage, along with a similarly sized can of dog food. The color and texture of both products have an uncanny resemblance; visually you can hardly tell the difference. Taste was to be the deciding factor.

This was to be a double blind test, in that both George and Wayne were blind to what was going on. The rest of us knew; they didn't.

Taking a razor blade and a tube of glue, Jim carefully removed the label from the dog food and replaced it with the one from the Banner Sausage. It was a skillful piece of work, I must say. The label showed no signs of having been tampered with, and, because both cans were the same size, if fit perfectly.

The rest of us were eager for breakfast the next morning, eager to see if the two aficionados could tell the difference. But fate intervened.

In all our years of camping, nothing had ever been stolen from our campsite. For that matter, nothing has ever been stolen since. But on that occasion, someone came through camp while all of us were fishing and stole one of our grocery bags. And yes, sad to say, it was the one containing the relabeled dog food.

We regretted not being able to conduct our carefully planned experiment, but it was just as much fun letting George and Wayne join us in speculating on how the thieves might be enjoying their fried Alpo. It was also the occasion for much theological discussion. As we contemplated the bastards getting their just desserts, we couldn't help but wonder: could there really be a god of justice? The best outcome, though, was that Banner Sausage never made another appearance, and George and Wayne never said a word.

⌒——ᴎ

Having fresh game on the camp menu—other than what might be frozen and brought along—is an annual possibility that has turned into one of those practiced rituals we observe but don't expect much from anymore, like electing someone who promises that our taxes will go down.

On our spring trips, Jim brings his shotgun, box caller, and camouflage so he can spend a few mornings gobbler hunting. He gets up around four a.m., long before the sun comes up, clunks down the stairs in his heavy boots, and makes more noise than a Maine moose before he finishes his coffee and takes up a position where he hopes some horny gobbler will wander by. He returns midmorning, consistently empty-handed.

Another version of this ritual takes place in the fall, when Jim goes out in the evening to deer hunt. As with the spring foray, he inevitably returns having inflicted no harm on the deer population. So accustomed have we become to his unproductive efforts that we have recently been asking him what he *really* does out there in the woods when he says he's hunting. You have to wonder.

The one time Jim did get his deer—it's been so long ago I nearly forgot—he realized that his deer stamp had expired. Knowing this contretemps could prove embarrassing for an outdoor writer, he prevailed on Dave and me to make a mad dash to buy him one. This would, of course, require one of us pretending to be Jim while making the purchase.

We pulled up outside a convenience store that sold hunting licenses and hurried inside while Jim waited back at the carcass—he couldn't check in his deer and be legal without the stamp. Dave confidently stepped up to the counter and in his usual perky voice told the clerk he wanted to purchase a deer stamp, commencing his role as Jim.

As the clerk was filling out the forms, I turned away from the counter and saw a state trooper sitting at a nearby table hunched over a sandwich and soda. He was close enough to hear clearly the interaction between Dave and the clerk, which got complicated when she asked certain questions Dave struggled to answer: Date of birth? What's that address again? Did you say your eyes are brown? *Dave is beginning to sound suspicious!* I thought.

Fear gripped my solar plexus as I envisioned myself behind bars, my clerical career in tatters, arrested for being an accessory to false impersonation. But Dave maintained his characteristic cool, and the clerk eventually filled in all the blanks and slid the deer stamp across the counter.

Throughout all this, the trooper remained occupied with his meal and paid no attention to us. As I remember, and it is hard to look back through a veil of fear, I don't recall that he even looked our way. But I was relieved and happy as a parolee to scurry out the door.

When we arrived back at camp, I was still feeling like a fugitive from justice and needed a stiff drink to settle my nerves. Dave, on the other hand, found the whole thing a hoot and had great fun recounting every detail.

What Jim lacks as a hunter he makes up for in the kitchen. He plans the menus, purchases all the food, and cooks the evening meals. Wayne, a chronic early riser, is the breakfast cook, and lunch is on our own. Jim purchases plenty of snack foods, so before we head out for the day we toss an assortment of sandwiches, candy bars, fruit, beef jerky, Nabs, potato chips, nuts, and trail mix into a sack to hold us till the evening meal.

A problem with snacks is that they can be so detrimental to your appearance, and by that I don't just mean the pounds they might add. One gorgeous fall day, three of us decided to drive over to The Homestead, a swanky resort in Hot Springs, Virginia, and pay the fee to fish the Cascades, a brisk little freestone stream that runs between two of the hotel's plush eighteen-hole golf courses.

The Cascades is not remote, but the hotel has kept its natural habitat relatively undisturbed. Towering hardwoods cover the sides of the valley through which it flows, and, reflective of its name, the Cascades angles sharply downward through a series of dramatic falls where it turns to lacy foam against the mammoth boulders worn smooth from its passing. The stream—and its surroundings—is a place of beauty in any season. Consequently, it's also a tourist attraction.

The resort has created a well-maintained trail along the stream and offers guided nature walks to its guests. Those interested are bussed over from the hotel in vans; groups of a dozen or so are led by their guides, who stop intermittently to deliver mini lectures on some aspect of geology, flora, or wildlife.

My buddies and I had spread out to fish the stream that morning, and had regrouped for lunch when a group of tourists came in view along the path. The van was parked near our truck, indicating that the tour was over and they would be heading back.

I had taken a seat on a fat log and pulled a can of pudding from the snack bag. Whoever had packed our lunch had forgotten to include any silverware, so I had to improvise and use the pull-top lid as a makeshift spoon. This worked OK, but it wasn't a precision instrument. In digging into the pudding can, I couldn't help dribbling some of the gooey yellow stuff on my beard.

I listened to the tourists jabbering in rapid conversation as they passed by on their way to the van, and thought to myself: *They sound like they might be from New York.* Which was OK—mind you, I am not prejudiced. At least I wasn't up until then.

Now I will admit that squatting on that log with pudding hanging from my beard, struggling with my prehensile skills to manipulate that can lid, didn't cause me to resemble the refined professional gentleman I am. But that was no excuse.

Before I had a chance to render myself more respectable, a guy bolted from the van, squatted not six feet from my face, and with his fancy German camera snapped off several shots of me hunkered down on that log eating pudding like a chimpanzee. He didn't say a word, just got his pictures, then turned and bolted for the van. The door folded shut before his feet hit the top step, and I could see him plopping into his seat with a fat grin on his face as the van pulled away. I guess he thought he had photographed a genuine mountain man. If he only knew.

Dinner is our main meal, and it's Jim's chance to show off his culinary stuff. It begins with cocktails on the covered porch, where we lean against the railing or kick back in the big wooden rockers while carrying on telling stories we wouldn't want repeated in polite company. At some point Jim will show up with a plate of hors d'oeuvres—shrimp cocktail or cheeses or pepperoni rolls or—like this last trip—a steaming plate of sautéed scallops, each encircled with a strip of fried bacon held in place with a toothpick used to lift them to our eager mouths.

When the main course is ready, we move inside, where Jim already has the table set. We eat off china now; no more crowding around a campfire eating on our laps. Most evenings, someone even volunteers to say grace before we sit down to stuff our faces, and stuff we do.

If Jim has a fault as a camp cook, it's that he cooks too much. Just imagine that you are looking at one of our most recent meals: A mounded salad bowl sits beside each plate. Several bottles of wine of varying shades stand ready to fill the crystal goblets donated by George from some extras he brought from home. A baked potato the size of a small football is on each plate; tubs of butter and sour cream wait nearby. Jim is trying to find a place to set down two glistening loaves of garlic bread he has just pulled from the oven.

All day, a pot of collards, cooked with a hock of ham, has simmered on the stove. To each plate a heap of these is added, and a serving of pinto beans is ladled on beside.

The main course this evening is beef tenderloin, each juicy piece cut in sections as thick as a two-by-four. At other times, Jim has smoked dozens of trout, served capons stuffed with rice, deep-fried an entire turkey, grilled steaks the size of dinner plates, and prepared roasts as long as your arm.

When the plates are clean (not many of those), there is plenty more for seconds...or thirds...and enough left over to feed the Pittsburgh Steelers.

Dessert follows. If you are not in the mood for cake, there are ice cream, cookies, fruit (nice idea but seldom chosen), and enough candy for Halloween. And the meal is still not over.

After dessert, depending on the weather, we waddle either to the porch or to the den, where George opens his humidor and offers some pretty upscale cigars for those who wish to partake. Jim comes along in a few minutes with a tray of after-dinner drinks—a blend of coffee liqueur and thick, rich cream is the usual offering, but there have been exceptions.

Bloated like gravid cows, we sink into our chairs. Conversation soon fades as our chins drift toward our chests, and gradually, one by one, we nod off.

Knowing all this, is it really so hard to understand why John puts on ten pounds whenever we get together for a little food and fellowship?

FAVORED RIVERS

Ask any fishermen who have been at it as long as we have, and they will quickly list their favorite rivers and streams. After years of experience, a few stand out above all the rest, like those exceptional people you meet in life, the ones you know you will never forget. And the simile isn't all that disconnected: a good river that has treated you well is right up there with a trusted friend.

For Dave, Bill, and me, a river that sits near the top of our lists is the Elk, in southeastern West Virginia— which is a little ironic in that we don't fish it all that often, certainly not nearly as often as we would like. The distinction is even more noteworthy when you consider the stiff competition from other rivers we have fished, including some of the most celebrated, in the U.S. and abroad.

I can't even remember exactly when it was that we started fishing the Elk. The first trip must have had something of an afterthought about it, because I don't remember hearing a lot about the Elk, and it was never on my rivers-yet-to-fish list.

Way back, the three of us used to make an annual trip to the Shavers Fork of the Cheat River. That was in the day when we still enjoyed roughing it, and drove our four-wheel-drive trucks deep into the woods on old logging roads so we could camp along the riverbanks. The fishing must have been slow on one of those trips, and we drove over to the Elk in search of more productive water.

Whatever the original reason that got us there, we found it, tried it, loved it; and it eventually became one of our favorite streams. Meanwhile, the Shavers Fork slipped into memory, and we haven't been back in years.

Each June the three of us make a four-day trip to the Elk, hoping to time it right to catch the annual green drake hatch, which is never a precision call: the hatch comes off in the spring, but weather can alter its predicted arrival by a couple of weeks, one way or the other. Most years we have arrived on time, if not for the peak of the hatch, at least in time to see a few of these gangly bugs, and to deceive some of the trout that fancy them with our feathery imitations.

It's roughly a four-hour drive to the Elk from our homes in Southwestern Virginia. I say "roughly" because Dave affects our driving time in much the same way the weather influences the arrival of the green drakes. What I mean is this: our arrival time depends on how often we stop, and most especially, as far as Dave is concerned, where we stop.

Bill and I—and we know from the get-go not to set our expectations too high—try to keep Dave's social encounters to a minimum. The effort is a lot like fighting a cold you already have but at least wanting to minimize the symptoms.

The primary objective is to keep Dave away from as many yard sales and antique stores as possible. Because he is a collector of antique fishing lures (with a nationally recognized collection), Dave is always scanning the roadsides for the possibility of a rare find, such as a yard sale where unknowing offspring have placed their grand-father's moldering tackle box—the one they found while cleaning out the attic of the old home place—on a display table with a five-dollar price tag attached.

It would not be so bad if he only stopped and looked. But Dave is incapable of stopping and looking. For Dave, stopping means talking, being sociable, making new friends—all of which takes awhile.

White Sulphur Springs is a particularly high-risk area. Dave grew up in nearby Lewisburg, and White Sulphur Springs is one of the places he used to frequent. The result is a history of old bars and old girlfriends, that sort of thing. If we don't make it through town without stopping, there is a high probability Dave will run into someone he knows, or someone who knows someone he used to know, and Bill and I will have to make yet another adjustment in our estimated time of arrival on the Elk.

Eventually, we get there. The last twenty miles—Route 219 between Marlinton and Slatyfork—are a short course on the reason West Virginia is renowned for its mountain roads. The grade is steep and twists and turns more than a veteran politician. If the state had not thought to add passing lanes in some of the sharpest hairpin turns, you could get stuck behind a stacked-high logging truck straining up the mountain at walking speed, and creep along back there for miles.

Roller-coaster ride is the overused description for such roads, but I can think of none better. They rise and fall and roll to one side, then the other. If you are prone to motion sickness, beware. But there is a consolation: if you are not in a hurry, the scenery is arresting—angular, verdant, and primal. West Virginia does not call itself "wild and wonderful" for no good reason.

We make one last stop in Marlinton before starting up the mountain. We stop there to get West Virginia fishing licenses, but on one occasion we also looked for a place to eat—Dave must have gabbed more than usual and extended our drive time way past lunch. The clerk in the outdoor store directed us to a simple building perched on the side of a hill overlooking the Greenbrier River.

Our first meal there was a plate of liver and onions so tender we could cut it with our forks. Another time, we had pot roast with chunks of beef as big as our fists. There have always been plenty of vegetables on the side, and cobbler of one kind or another for dessert. And each time we've paid our bills, there's been change left over from a ten.

Stopping there is now an expectation, and we count on it. And while that small insertion into our routine may indicate how long we have been making our journey to the Elk, more importantly it provides a discreet example of how good buddies build rituals into their ventures that become every bit as important as the fishing they claim is the purpose of the trip.

Dave, Bill, and I gave up camping when we started fishing the Elk, and over the years we have been through a series of rented cabins, each change bringing us closer to the water. For the past few years, we have rented a cabin in Elk Springs that is so close to the river that from the front porch we can watch trout rise and we can listen to the water sing as we fall asleep at night.

It is the special regulation section between Slatyfork and Elk Springs that keeps us coming back. To us it represents fishing as it used to be—or at least as we like to think it used to be—before pollution and environmental degradation reduced mountain trout streams from their original pristine state.

Trout on the Elk are wild and savvy, and I am convinced their feral character connects us with something primitive within ourselves. They also require a tiring physical effort to get to the ones that haunt our favorite places on the river. We three prefer to walk a good way before stringing up our rods, to put distance between ourselves and the convenient, heavily fished areas that are a ten-minute stroll from the nearest parking spots.

An old railroad line, rusted and long inactive, parallels the Elk, a remnant of the heavy logging and mining days. For nearly an hour we follow the tracks and the weedy paths that appear intermittently alongside. This gets us deeper into the special reg area—and the forest—where other fishermen are far less likely to be seen. Frequently we have stumbled down the embankment from the tracks, waded through hat-high grass to reach a certain pool, and fished till dark without ever seeing another soul.

There are, however, trade-offs for this solitude. When we fish past sunset, it is a long walk back in the dark. And, as Dave says, we have to keep an eye out for "Johnny No Shoulders."

The daylight sun warms the track beds, a favorite lounging spot for coldblooded snakes looking to soak up a little heat. On our trip out, we switch on tiny lamps attached to the bills of our caps and sweep the beams of hand-held flashlights across our path. Treading on a resting viper is no way to end a good day of fishing, and there are enough rattlesnakes and copperheads in the mountains around the Elk to make us care about where we plant our feet.

Falling is a peril that many fishermen underestimate on any given outing. On the Elk, the possibilities increase. Because the tracks along the river have been so long neglected, there are places where the bed beneath them has been washed away by periodic floods. Such places are few in number, and the span is usually short. Nevertheless, where they occur, traversing them is like stepping along an outsize horizontal ladder, where nothing but air fills the spaces between the weather-beaten ties that hang by spike heads from the bottom of the rails and wobble beneath your boots when you press your weight on them. We step gingerly as we cross, sometimes not wanting to look down to the floor of the gap that can be as much as twenty or thirty feet below.

On one of our recent trips, we walked a mile or so before we started dropping off at likely holding spots along the river. Bill was the first to step off the tracks and onto the steep bank that slanted down to the river. Dave and I continued on for another quarter-mile before he got in. After an additional half-mile or so, I did the same. As is our custom, we had agreed on a specific time and place to meet—in three hours, at the spot where Bill had started to fish. In the meantime, each of us would be on his own, out of contact and out of sight.

It was near time to regroup; I was moving downriver, making a few more casts before climbing back up on the tracks, when Dave appeared. We walked back together, and as we rounded the final bend we could see Bill in the distance, leaning awkwardly to the side, supporting himself with a sturdy branch.

Only minutes after Dave and I had left him, Bill had stumbled while moving along the steep, rock-covered bank. His right leg folded under him as the bulk of his weight fell hard on the knee. Bill's a big man, and a tough one, too, but he nearly passed out from the pain and thought at first he'd broken his leg.

The pain subsided enough for Bill to drag himself up the hill, where he found the stick that Dave and I saw him leaning against as he came into view. Fortunately, the leg turned out not to be broken: the doctor said severely strained. It was bad enough, though...bad enough to end Bill's fishing for that trip. And it could have been worse, much worse. As a consequence, we now stick pocket-size walkie-talkies in our vests. They won't keep us from falling, but at least we can call for help. That's a lot better than waiting hours for someone to happen by, which can easily happen on the Elk.

The Elk runs through limestone country, a geological phenomenon that results in a pH level conducive to varied and prolific insect life. It also creates an interesting limnological situation, wherein sections of the Elk disappear, seeping through the porous rock strata to continue flowing underground. This is particularly so during periods of dry weather.

There is one section of the Elk—descriptively known as "The Dries"—that is sometimes present, and sometimes not. Because The Dries is devoid of water much of the year, the fish do not set up housekeeping there. During these barren periods, the water travels beneath the stream-bed, resurfacing at Elk Springs, where it once again becomes a fishable stream.

In the early spring, if there has been sufficient snow-melt and ground-swelling rain, water in The Dries will run aboveground along a twisting, rock-strewn course. To look at it during such times, you would think it the ideal habitat for trout. Many a visiting angler has thought so and been deceived.

There was a fellow we met who had driven down from somewhere up north during the early spring when plenty of water was flashing through The Dries. As we passed, he was making studied casts to what he thought would be a likely holding spot. We pulled over and explained why he was wasting his time. Ultimately, he was grateful for the advice, but we could hardly fault him for his initial distrust. I mean, think of how it must have looked: three guys in a truck with North Carolina license plates drive up and say there are no fish where he is fishing because the river disappears. It does sound like a leg-puller if you think about it.

On our June trip, in addition to the green drakes, we can usually count on seeing light Cahills, stoneflies, sulfurs, blue winged olives, caddis, mahogany duns, March browns, gray foxes, and sundry other emerging flies. Despite the abundance of insect life, Elk River trout are not easily fooled. When a hatch is on, you had better match it, and even having a good facsimile attached to the end of your tippet is no guarantee of success. To complicate matters, there are times—particularly in midafternoon—when you might be fooled into thinking there aren't very many fish in the Elk. During the middle of the day, the fishing can be slow. But just wait until the last hour before dark.

That's our favorite time to fish. That's when the river explodes into life. That's when we make the trek to one of our favorite spots, where we wait with rods tucked under our arms as the sun slips below the ridgeline and gray shadows slide down from the surrounding hills. That's the time when the fishing is at its best.

The first indication will be a rise or two along the far bank. Looking up, we will see swarms of spinners gathering in the darkening sky to perform their copulating dance before descending to the water to lay their eggs and die. Soon, their spent bodies with outstretched wings will dot the surface as the rising of the trout picks up pace.

During these spinner falls, we have had some of our best fishing…anywhere. It can be exciting, challenging, and sometimes frustrating—especially when trout are rising all around and seem completely uninterested in any fly we show them. But it all comes in just the right proportions to keep us coming back for more.

As with most memorable rivers, it is not just the quality of fishing that places the Elk on our A-list—although, and I have to be honest here, that has a lot to do with it. Still, we have to factor in other considerations, such as the camaraderie and the stories we have accumulated throughout all the years of going there. Like the one Bill tells about the evening he caught a 24 ½-inch brown and Dave and I didn't catch squat. But I'll skip the details; Dave and I don't like that story.

Then there is the scenery. Oh yes, the scenery. West Virginia, despite the ravages of certain industries, is a state of distinctive natural beauty. The flora and fauna of the hardwood mountain forests are spectacular in their abundance and diversity.

Along the trails we have walked, we have passed wildflowers of every hue. Once we stopped to let a hen turkey trailing eight newly hatched chicks cut across our path. We have interrupted our fishing to watch slim, dark otters slide off the riverbanks, and more than once been evicted from pools by tail-slapping beavers signaling that we had waded too close to their dens.

We have listened to grouse drum atop rotting stumps, and tilted our necks skyward to watch hawks, eagles, ducks, and osprey circle high above our heads. Bears have lumbered by, including a mother leading three scrambling little cubs—a rare sighting, since a female seldom has so many young. But we were in West Virginia, where we have learned not to be surprised by what may be rare in other places.

The quality of the fishing and the environs of West Virginia are impressive, and they are a big part of why we keep returning to the Elk. But so are the friendships we have made, and not just with one another. As I was writing this chapter, I learned of the death of one of our favorite Elk River friends.

I can't remember when we first met the legendary Charlie Heartwell. Dave—as you might imagine—was the first to make Charlie's acquaintance and introduced him to Bill and me. Entomologist, fly tier extraordinaire—creator of a commercial line of flies known as "Charlie's Charmers"—master angler, trout specialist, raconteur, and all-around great guy. We looked forward to connecting with Charlie on every trip. We weren't always successful, but we will definitely remember our last visit with him…especially since it was our last.

We had invited Charlie to join us for some evening fishing and a steak dinner after. He said he wasn't up to the fishing, but he'd be happy to take us up on the steak.

He met us at the cabin one evening, and we had a memorable meal together. Bill was commended for grilling the steaks to each man's specifications, but the real *piece de resistance* that evening was Charlie.

Charlie was an expansive presence with a jovial manner and a hearty laugh. He was a talker, too. But unlike a lot of talkers, he didn't wear you out. You just kept hoping he'd go on.

Bill, Dave, and I sat forward in our chairs and listened like attentive schoolchildren gathered around their favorite teacher as Charlie entertained us with one story after another. We savored every tasty anecdote, every scrap of fishing wisdom, every morsel of Elk River lore he served up that night.

Charlie was an expert on the Elk River, but he was even more of an expert on the insects that live there. Outside the cabin door that night, a dense cobweb encircling the porch light had ensnared an impressive collection of unfortunate mayflies that had been drawn in by the gleaming bulb. Eager to know exactly what was hatching, we asked: "Charlie, can you identify any of these?" What a silly question that was.

Leaning into the light, peering over the top of his bifocals, his demeanor noticeably shifting to that of the serious scholar, Charlie convened a seminar, delivering an amazingly detailed and scientific lecture on the various species entangled in the thin fibers of the web.

"Now this is *Ephemerella dorothea,* female dun," he said, pointing to one of the little yellow specimens. And so it went, as Charlie stood in the beam of the porch light enlightening us on the subtleties of color, recent changes in entomological classifications, and specific behavioral characteristics of the insects under examination—using assigned Latin terms as well as the corresponding common names of their most frequently used artificial imitations.

Listening to Charlie that evening was like being in a college classroom—an enjoyable one. And when he finally wrapped it up, his audience gaped at one another with that wide-eyed look of "wow" on our faces; not to mention gratitude for certain bits of information that would serve us well in our future engagements with the finicky Elk River trout.

I have no doubt that on some future occasion, when we are relaxing on the porch that served as Charlie's podium, enjoying a drink while we wait for Bill to finish grilling a thick slab of deer tenderloin, we will lift our glasses to Charlie. He's become part of the whole package of the Elk River experience. And we sure are going to miss him.

In the end, I am not sure what criteria I would recommend for deciding on a favorite river. The longer the boys and I fish, the more the qualifications seem to change and our attitudes tend to shift. Maybe it's like a long-term marriage, where the paramount reasons for getting married aren't necessarily the same ones we would cite for staying so.

For sure, deciding on a favorite river is a subjective experience. And as the years pass, the determination becomes even more complex as a growing list of multi-factorial considerations complicate the task.

Thinking about it too much gives me a headache, which is contrary to why I fish in the first place. When I am on the water, I don't want to have to think too much, or even do too much—I already have enough of that. I just want to be, and enjoy the world around me. But I have compiled a few thoughts. You can take them or leave them; in the end it will be your own considerations that matter in determining a favorite river, whatever they may be.

But here's what works for me: A favorite river is a place where new friendships are formed and old ones deepened; where getting there is almost as much fun as being there; where stories flood our thoughts with memories of being there when circumstances determine that we cannot.

A favorite river is a place where we find what eludes us under the pressures of our daily doings. It is a place where we don't have to explain or make excuses or please or compromise or impress. It is a place that does not expect a lot from us, only that we honor and respect it. In return, it promises to reconnect us with the natural world from which we have too long been estranged.

A favorite river is a place where we make history, our own personal history. It is a place that becomes a part of us, and we a part of it. It is a home, maybe our real home, where we are what we always thought ourselves to be: the person we hope still lives and thrives beneath the counterfeit selves we parade before the world.

A favorite river is a place of peace and contentment. It is a place that brings out the best in us and makes us glad at the end of the day that we chose to be there.

Well, as you can see, it *is* possible to think too much about such things. Sometimes, it seems, for those of us who value rivers and what they do for us, we just can't help ourselves. So I'll leave it at that, with just one final comment: If a river becomes a favorite, you will know it. You just will. It is like falling in love. And like falling in love, in retrospect it might prove interesting to ponder the reasons why. But they won't matter. They won't matter because you will have already felt the reason why, somewhere in the vicinity of your heart. That's why I am sitting here getting all excited about our next excursion to the Elk.

THE AMBIVALENCE OF STUFF

The holiday season has arrived, and my wife and I bought two Christmas trees this year. "Enough," she said, "the fishing ornaments are taking over; they need a tree of their own."

It was a good suggestion. So, while the fishing tree is smaller than the family model, and not nearly as elegant, it looks pretty sharp decorated with those miniature waders and creels; Santa Clauses holding fly rods; ornamental fish of various colors, poses, and materials; oversize gaudy flies encased in clear glass globes; a tiny fishing hat; itsy-bitsy canoes; two small wooden "gone fishing" signs; a treetop angel complete with rod; and…well, you can see why we needed a second tree.

All of this is a result of years of acquisition, and not much of it my own doing, I want you to know. I have been stereotyped. Whenever someone thinks about giving me a gift, finding something "fishing" becomes the shopper's modus operandi.

Before retiring from the church I served for twenty-seven years, parishioners would show their gratitude during the holiday season with gifts of appreciation. That was the source of most of my fish-related ornaments. I am not complaining: I love those ornaments—mostly because they remind me of the people who gave them. But over the years, I received so many I ended up with duplicates and had to adopt some out to buddies who promised to give them a decent home.

And it doesn't end with the ornaments. I have enough fish-themed neckties and T-shirts to open a small boutique. There are the mugs in the cabinet with slogans like "Fishermen have great rods" printed on their sides, and designer cushions so thick I have to toss them from my reading chair to make enough room to sit.

As I write here in my basement office, I notice the coaster beneath my water glass bearing the picture of a leaping trout. It is one of a six-item set; the other five are scattered throughout the house. To my right, the pad for my computer's mouse displays the colorful images of an angler's vest and landing net.

On the bookshelf behind the desk sits a long ceramic fish, concave and bowl-like, made to hold a serving spoon. I didn't know where else to put it. My wife said she didn't want that thing in her kitchen, and it does somewhat match the decorative plate propped next to it that has three bas relief fish swimming across its face.

A foot-tall wooden nutcracker, all decked out in fishing garb, resides on another shelf—Tchaikovsky would swoon—opposite a rectangular, metal candy tin with the picture of a rainbow trout on top and "Good Catch" written on the front and back. The stapler with the fish-shaped stapling arm is an item of curiosity to visitors (just whack that rainbow smartly on the head), as is the light switch cover with the painted brook trout on its surface. Upstairs there are two wall-socket plates bearing a similar design.

Then there are the bathroom items: fishy trash can, towels, and shower curtain, all of which go nicely with the four-slot toothbrush holder in the shape of a creel.

OK, you get the picture. There is no end to this stuff; it's everywhere I look.

And these are just samplings of some gifts that came my way. If I were to inventory all the fishing tackle, fly-tying equipment, rods, reels, vests, waders, clothes, books, and related fishing necessities I have acquired on my own over the past forty years, the situation would get really serious.

Who am I kidding—the situation got way past serious a long time ago. In fact, my wife laid down the law a couple of years ago and declared a fishing-item-free zone in our house—like a nonsmoking section. She feared guests might mistake our home for a fishing lodge.

The living room, the guest room, our bedroom, and the kitchen are now off-limits. There is special dispensation for the newly designated "fishing tree," but only for the Christmas season. The remaining rooms—as of this writing, anyway—still display an array of lamps, prints, wood carvings, watercolors, figurines, photographs, antique tackle, and assorted memorabilia of a distinctively angling nature.

I don't know where I heard the story, and I can't vouch for either its accuracy or its authenticity, but it's a story I can appreciate. As it was told to me, the wife of a fishing guide went to the couple's basement one day and decided to count the number of fishing rods her husband kept down there. "I counted fifty rods," she complained. Upon hearing the news, he gasped with astonishment: "My God, someone's broken in and stolen half of them."

No, I don't have fifty fly rods. And no, I am not going to tell you how many I do have. Do you really expect me to put that kind of incriminating information in print? Still, I have a lot of stuff.

The early days were simpler, partly because I couldn't afford a lot of extraneous gear, but mainly because there wasn't nearly as much of it around to buy. It seems that, back then, most of us were satisfied with just a few basics. A functional vest, a pair of boot-foot canvas waders, and a good all-around rod and reel about did it. Maybe you had two rods if you had some extra cash and were really serious about the sport. That's hardly the case today.

Fishing catalogs that were thin and few in number forty years ago are now thick, glossy, and too numerous to keep up with. Some are the equal of fashion magazines and market their wares in much the same way. Why, some of the new fishing vests are as elegant as Armani suits, with price tags to match.

It seems almost comical that some tackle companies debut a new line of rods each year—sleeker, stiffer models made of the latest generation of carbon fibers, purporting to cast a line farther and faster than last year's passé pole. They often showcase the advanced metallurgy of the line guides or the elegance of reel seats made from exotic woods. I wouldn't be surprised to see slender Parisian models carrying them down a catwalk at some annual rod and tackle show.

Come on. How pretty do these things need to be? And are we to think that the possibility of casting an extra foot or two is going to make a significant difference in how competent an angler we become? Maybe the question we really need to ask—and I include my obviously guilty self here—is: Whom are we trying to impress with our fancy high-end gear?

There is a historic recession going on right now that came within a catfish's whisker of dropping our economy and our country into another Great Depression. If anything good has emerged from the experience, it may be that many of us are beginning to think more about our stuff, and whether it makes sense to keep adding to the pile. Isn't that what got us into this current financial mess?

When I started tying flies, I began with a serviceable but inexpensive vise. As the years passed, I kept trading up, acquiring ever more expensive vices. (Now there's a revealing double-entendre I didn't see coming!) The essential thing any of them had to do was firmly hold a hook in place, which all of them did quite well. The rotating, interchangeable jaws and other add-on features of the newer vices are nice, but they aren't the deciding factor when it comes to tying better flies.

I don't mean to imply that excessive purchasing of fishing equipment was a contributor to our nation's financial meltdown; that would be silly. But taking an objective look at what we have—even if it's just fishing gear—is a good indicator of how we relate to stuff in general. In a world of finite resources, the question "How much is enough?" is still an estimable one. And while it may not have featured prominently in their MBA exams, I wish certain Wall Street executives would have at least given it a passing nod.

No question about it, I own a mountain more of gear than when my father and I headed for the pier with two rods, a galvanized minnow bucket, and a packet of hooks in hand. A lot of the new products I enjoy, and some of them, such as clothes made from space-age fibers, make my days on the water longer and a whole lot more pleasant.

But I doubt that I enjoy fishing more now than when I was a kid. And even if I do, the extra stuff is not what makes the difference.

Most of what I own I don't need; and most of what I want I don't need. It was a bit unnerving when I took stock of all the paraphernalia I have bought over the years and realized how much of it I've never used…or worse, forced myself to use so I could justify the purchase. At some point I convinced myself—or was advertised into the conviction—that I had to have it. The irony in all of this is that the lust for acquisitions is behind the attitude that is destroying the "good life" we so ardently pursue.

So, the question "How much is enough?" is chafing my conscience these days as I ponder whether there will be enough resources left should my grandchildren wish to enjoy the pleasures that fly-fishing has afforded me. The question was particularly hard to avoid as I was hanging ornaments on the Christmas fishing tree this year.

Maybe all this fuming will motivate me to do something about it. Maybe I could forgo my next needless purchase and give the money to a conservation group. Maybe I could simplify, get real about what I need and what I don't, and share some of the excess with a kid who is just getting started in the sport. Maybe I could make a difference simply by thinking about—and maybe even changing—my attitude about my stuff.

Meanwhile, if any family or friends are thinking about getting me a Christmas gift this year: nothing with fish on it. PLEASE. How about a check to Trout Unlimited instead?

Carpe Diem

The first time I saw the big brown was in late spring. Actually, what I saw were large rings fanning out from the spot where it had breached the surface. As I watched them pile up like waves along the shoreline, I knew that only a fish of considerable heft could generate rings of that size.

It was too late to make a cast: the fish had spotted me and was already heading for cover, its dorsal fin cutting a V-shaped wake as it sped away and disappeared.

I was fishing a brisk little freestone stream in western North Carolina that ran through private land. And because it was posted *and* patrolled, only family members and a few special guests ever got to fish there. Legally, that is.

The family had granted me fishing rights shortly after I became rector of St. Mary's Church in High Point— their church. And throughout the twenty-seven years I served the congregation at St. Mary's, I fished that little stream enough to know it intimately and well. It remains the best small mountain stream I have ever fished.

For such a modest stream, it harbored some impressive trout. I had caught enough to know. They weren't monsters, and I didn't catch the big ones with any regularity; but the clean water, abundant insect life, and low fishing pressure allowed for the possibility of trophy-sized fish.

When I saw the massive swirl, I knew I was dealing with what might possibly be the biggest fish in the stream, certainly the biggest I had ever encountered there.

The big fish presided over one of the largest pools in the stream. Oblong in shape, the pool's upper end bordered a long stretch of rock-strewn riffles—the optimum delivery system for aquatic life and other stream-borne food. All a hungry fish had to do was hang back and wait for dinner to be served.

Along one bank, the water was no more than a few inches deep. From there, the streambed tapered down and away, forming a deep depression against the opposite bank, over which hung a thick canopy of rhododendron with leaves so low they skimmed the surface. It was the perfect arrangement for protection and escape, and there is where the big trout lived.

That summer I made frequent trips to the mountains, and my desire to catch that fish intensified with each failed attempt. There were occasions when I would see it taking insects off the surface and thought I might get lucky. But the wary trout would either see me creeping toward its pool or be startled by the presentation of my fly, and cruise away.

At other times, there would be no signs of it at all, and I would wonder if it had been killed by a mink or otter, or, worse yet, been caught by someone else.

Eventually, I got a good look at the fish and had to revise upward my initial assessment of its size. It was early evening, and the fading sunlight struck the clear water at just the right angle to illuminate the fish's dark shadow moving across the pool. It was well over two feet long. That's a big trout in any water. In a small mountain stream, that's the fish of a lifetime.

For months I tried every trick I knew to catch that fish, with no success. Once it took my fly in a violent boil of water, then tore off into the low-hanging rhododendron and broke me off. It was obvious why the fish had grown to such a size: it had an easily accessible supply of food and high-security protection; but most of all, it had experience and was full of guile.

I often thought about that fish back in my High Point office, a hundred miles away, supposedly preoccupied with other things. I began to feel like Ahab, obsessed with my giant fish.

Let me point out that there had been a lot of fish in my life up to that point, including some caught in Alaska that would have dwarfed even this one. But for some reason this fish became special; and I was driven to pursue it. Only later would I know why.

It was a gray, mid-November day when I drove to the mountains for what I knew would be my last shot at the fish until the following spring. Temperatures were dropping, and it would not be long until anchor ice formed along the stream banks and the metabolism of the fish would slow to where it hardly fed at all.

When I got to the pool, a layer of fallen leaves floated on the surface like a flotilla of little brown rafts, so many I thought of not even bothering. Not only would a cast have to land cleanly in an open spot, but the disturbance caused by a hooked leaf—not an unlikely possibility— would mean game over, forget about another cast.

As I was pondering what to do, a gentle rise swelled from one of the clear spots between the leaves. It was not dramatic, and even made me wonder if it could have been made by a smaller fish...not my fish. But it was late in the season, and I had nothing to lose.

The only insects I thought likely to be on the water would be terrestrials, so I tied on a large black beetle. Crawling on my hands and knees through the shallow water where the pool tailed out, I got as close as I dared, keeping my profile low to the ground.

Once in place, I made the cast, the only one I was likely to get. As the fly dropped into the circle of open water where the dimple had appeared, I still had no idea if it had been made by the fish of my dreams, or another.

A fragment of a second, attenuated and filled with expectation, stretched between the settling of the fly and the bulging of the surface. The fly was there and then it wasn't. It disappeared into the large brown head, and the line tightened against the fish's downward arc. The great fish was hooked.

It tugged against the pressure and made two small head-shaking circles before turning toward the rhododendron and the deep water beneath. Having once lost the fish in the tangle of those branches, I bent the rod hard against its intended retreat. To my surprise, the fish stopped short and turned back toward the center of the pool.

After a few more listless circles, it lunged toward the bottom, lifting its fan-like tail above the surface as it headed down. Thrumming reverberated through the line as the big brown rubbed its nose against the rocks, trying to free the hook. It held, and the fish turned once again to the surface.

It was beginning to tire, noticeably, and far sooner than expected. I had caught much smaller fish that had put up a tougher fight, but this fish was clearly giving up, surrendering, and I was wondering why.

It made another gesture toward its lair, quickly gave in to the rod pressure, rolled over on the surface, and let me haul it in. I scooped the landing net—which turned out to be too small—then guided the fish toward the shallow water where I could block its escape and get my hands beneath its head and tail.

Carefully balancing its weight, I lifted the fish toward the surface. I wanted a good look at the creature that had haunted me for so many months, the fish I had thought about and pursued like no other fish before it. I wanted a face-to-face. I wanted to convey my regards, the way one does with an athletic opponent or business competitor one has come to admire and respect.

The fish lay calmly in my hands. Other than the gentle flaring of its gills, it did not move. Despite the brevity of our tussle, it was spent, exhausted. As I studied its long, dappled body, it was not hard to see why.

The great fish's girth was uncommonly lean for a fish so long. And while its massive head and hooked, predatory jaw indicated a once-muscular frame, the fish had fallen on hard times, which had clearly sapped its strength and reduced its size.

The preceding summer had been dry in the mountains of North Carolina, and the low water had made it difficult for the fish to find sufficient food to support its heavy frame. A large fish in a small stream is particularly susceptible to such conditions; and opportunities to move to other, more-sustaining pools are limited. In this fish's case, they were nonexistent. Stress had claimed its heavy toll.

I held the fish in my outstretched hands long enough to appreciate its beauty...and to be drawn into the glowing, lidless eye that stared back at mine. Yes, I know we humans project sentiments onto our hapless animal companions, assigning them all manner of feelings and thoughts of which they are in no way capable. (Just ask a devoted owner about the personality of his dog.) Nevertheless, the space between the fish's eye and mine was charged with intimacy. Maybe it was because I have known some lean and difficult times myself. Maybe it was because I, too, have worn out, become dispirited, and lost some fights I would have rather won. Whatever I projected onto the defeated fish in that brief flash of time and recognition, it stirred something deep within my soul.

In that moment, I wanted the great fish to survive. I wanted it to live, to enjoy more days in the sparkling pool beneath the deep blue dome of a Carolina sky. I wanted to return it to the place where it could hear the sound of water rushing through rocks, see the choreography of mayflies massing in conjugal dance, watch the descent of leaves scribing half-circle arcs in the autumn air, marvel at the explosion of bright colors from brown earth announcing the arrival of spring.

I felt in that moment as though a kindred spirit lay helpless and trusting in the curve of my hands. A poignant desire washed over me, a desire for both of us to continue on, to continue on together, at least for a while, for as long as the going-on might last. I wanted us to enjoy what filled us both with life and peace, with happiness and desire.

A quick twist of the hook popped it free, and I lowered the fish below the surface, holding it there until its gills spread in a steady rhythm, assuring me it had revived.

I opened my fingers and the fish rose; like a giant bird of prey, it lifted from my fingers, severing the contact between its flesh and mine. It slid away, and its long dark shadow moved slowly, steadily across the pool until it eased into the deep water beneath the overhanging leaves of the rhododendron and vanished.

It was spring before I returned to the little stream. Then, and several more times that summer, I slinked along the bank, and from a hidden place well back in the brush, I looked for signs of the great fish: a shadow like a drifting log; a wave-making swirl; a surface wake formed by a large cleaving tail. Nothing. I never saw the fish again, but I continue to wonder…and to hope.

When the boys and I reach the end of one of our extended trips, I have noticed that a predictable mood descends as we pack up and prepare to go our separate ways, as we get ready to transition back to the private worlds we escape during our intermittent times away. All of us are subdued. Conversation is sparse, the volume down a notch or two as each man busies himself with picking up around the lodge or getting his clothes and tackle together for the trip back home.

The deep stillness is not about the work or the anticipated fatigue of the highway miles ahead. Rather, I sense it has more to do with the act of leaving itself, the saying goodbye, which touches the deeper sentiments of death and loss that live within the human soul. Our trip-ending adieus are softer versions of harder goodbyes, rehearsals for ultimate endings: the letting-go of what we deeply love and can't imagine living without.

The lives my buddies and I now inhabit, like the rivers and streams we fish, are passing through time and place on a course to their final destinations. At their end, they will flow together, absorbed back into the great body of being from which all life began.

The boys and I have never talked of such things, but unspoken emotions speak their own silent message, and I have a strong suspicion that each one of them would nod in agreement with my words. We have been fishing buddies long enough that words sometimes are redundant, unnecessary for communicating what we already know and feel.

As a group, we have been long on the water and traveled far together. We have known adventure, compiled memories, and lost Ed along the way. Even so, we continue to delight in the sound of water slicing through the rocks, mayflies dancing in the air, leaves descending in the fall, bright colors spreading on brown earth in the spring…and great fish lurking in deep pools below the tangled leaves. And so we will, until each of us has made his final cast.

ACKNOWLEDGMENTS

Finishing a book generates a rainbow of emotions: accomplishment, satisfaction, and even relief that the job is done. But the dominant sentiment is gratitude for the part that others played in bringing your book to life. Without their help, you realize your book never would have reached completion. This was certainly true with Journey to the Final Cast and these are the people I wish to thank. The essential debt of gratitude goes to my fishing buddies who supplied the material for all that is written here—the accumulated experience, what was fit to print, of over thirty years of fishing together.

But more than the adventures shared over the past three decades, I value their friendship, perhaps more than they know. They are my boon companions. To Dave Gladwell, Steve Uhlin, Bill Bowen, John Savides, George Gillespie, Jim Brewer, Wayne Haga, and the late Ed Barbery, I express my utmost gratitude for all the ways in which you have enriched my life.

Writing is an arduous task in my case, benefited mightily from knowledgeable advisors. Marggie Graves edited my early drafts, offered suggestions, and saved me from many an egregious error. For her consummate skills and sage advice I am most grateful.

Several good friends read initial copies of the manuscript. They were an intentionally varied group, but mainly I chose them because they are perceptive readers whom

I trusted to give honest critiques. So, thank you Diane Cochran, Steve Uhlin, Mary Beth Yates, Tom Reisdorf, John Savides and Kathy Busch for the contributions you made to the final draft. All of you offered corrections, constructive criticism, and encouragement; because of you the book improved.

Joyce Maddox, my contact at Warwick House, is a rare combination of pleasant manner and extraordinary competence. She is a master copy editor: even the tiniest grammatical miscreants failed to sneak past her eagle eye. In addition to providing superb editing skills, Joyce, along with Amy Moore, nursed the manuscript through the myriad of technical details that eventually resulted in a book. Thank you, Warwick House. You are the best.

Credits for the cover design belong to Trisha Roth, a veritable fountain of creative ideas and artistic talent.

My deepest thanks go to Kathy Busch, my beloved wife of forty-one years. She encouraged me to write this account, supported me throughout the process, and indulged all that was necessary for these stories to take shape in the first place. Perhaps only the wives of inveterate fishermen will appreciate what that required. She is the love of my life, and every fishing trip was made all the brighter by knowing that her sweet smile would welcome my return.

Thank you, all of you. I could not have done it without you.

—Glenn E. Busch